How to Get Rich Exporting

Make it Big in the Export Business

By

Patrick W. Nee

(Patrick Nee)

The Internationalist®

The Internationalist®
International Business, Investment, and Travel

Published by:

The Internationalist Publishing Company

96 Walter Street/Suite 200

Boston MA 02131, USA

Tel: 617-354-7722

www.internationalist.com

PN@internationalist.com

Copyright © 2014 by PWN

The Internationalist is a Registered Trademark. How to Get Rich Exporting and The Internationalist Business Guides series are Trademarks of the Internationalist Publishing Company.

All rights are reserved under International, Pan-American, and Pan-Asian Conventions. No part of this book may be reproduced in any form without the written permission of the publisher. All rights vigorously enforced.

Welcome to **How to Get Rich Exporting**:

The key to a successful business is knowing the market. HOW TO GET RICH EXPORTING offers business owners, investors, and entrepreneurs all the need-to-know information to succeed in the field.

Written as an in-depth, straightforward reference guide, this book lists key information about the export market, its challenges, and opportunities. Readers will find information ranging from developing a strategy, implementing that strategy, pricing, shipping, and post-sale customer service.

HOW TO GET RICH EXPORTING is an instructive manual for those who want to expand their business—or start a new one—by exporting. It offers thorough information about the contemporary exports market.

Whether you are looking to break into international business or need to update your knowledge on modern-day exporting procedures and trade— this comprehensive guide is for you.

The Internationalist

Contents

Chapter 1: Introduction

Chapter 2: DEVELOPING AN EXPORT STRATEGY

Chapter 3: DEVELOPING A MARKETING PLAN

Chapter 4: EXPORT ADVICE

Chapter 5: METHODS AND CHANNELS

Chapter 6: FINDING QUALIFIED BUYERS

Chapter 7: USING TECHNOLOGY LICENSING AND JOINT VENTURES

Chapter 8: PREPARING YOUR PRODUCT FOR EXPORT

Chapter 9: EXPORTING SERVICES

Chapter 10: INTERNATIONAL LEGAL CONSIDERATIONS

Chapter 11: GOING ONLINE: E-EXPORTING TOOLS FOR SMALL BUSINESSES

Chapter 12: SHIPPING YOUR PRODUCT

Chapter 13: PRICING, QUOTATIONS, AND TERMS

Chapter 14: METHODS OF PAYMENT

Chapter 15: FINANCING EXPORT TRANSACTIONS

Chapter 16: BUSINESS TRAVEL ABROAD

Chapter 17: SELLING OVERSEAS AND AFTER-SALES SERVICE

Appendix: Glossary

Chapter 1: Introduction

THE WORLD IS OPEN FOR BUSINESS

In This Chapter

- **Selling globally is easier than ever.**
- **More help is available than ever.**
- **Your assumptions may not be accurate.**
- **You can transform your business—and yourself.**

The world is open for business: your business. Today it's easier than ever for a company like yours, regardless of size, to sell goods and services across the globe. Depending on what you're selling, with the right kind of phone directory for Toronto or Vancouver you can make sales calls and ship product to Canada tomorrow. In fact, more small U.S. companies sell to Canadian buyers than to buyers in any other country.

More U.S. small and medium-sized companies are exporting than ever before. In 2005, 232,600 small and medium-sized companies exported to a least one international market, a nearly 3 percent increase over 2004. The value of total goods and services exports grew almost 17 percent from 2009 to 2010, to more than $1.8 trillion. Your company may be included in these numbers but could sell even more. Or if your company hasn't made an international sale yet, yours could be the next one to sell globally.

If you have a Web presence, you have a global marketing and order-taking platform. For a few more dollars, you can process credit card payments for buyers in Australia or translate key pages into Spanish and other languages to further your reach. Easy.

Want more sales channels? Online marketplaces offer virtual storefronts and a ready-made global army of shoppers. They also offer payment solutions, and you can choose a shipper that will take care of the required documentation for you. The shippers want to help make things easier too, and many offer free international business advice, customer broker services, cost calculators, and financing. Plus, they'll pick up goods and documents from your back door and deliver them to almost any address in the world. And you can track everything on their Web site. Easy.

Want even more sales channels? If Web-based marketing and sales are insufficient to meet your sales growth appetite, you can attend trade shows in the United States where buyers from around the world come to purchase U.S. goods and services. Show organizers will facilitate introductions to the buyers, working with agencies of the U.S. government to provide matchmaking services on the show floor. These same government agencies can arrange for you to attend shows in other countries, where the connections and influence of your embassy network can save you time and money generating new business. Government agencies can find buyers for you and arrange introductions in more than 100 countries. Call this service "customized business matchmaking." Easy.

Today's global trading system is ideal for the smaller company employing more than one marketing and sales channel to sell into multiple overseas markets. But most U.S. exporters currently sell to one country market—Canada, for example. And the smaller the company, the less likely it is to export to more than one country. For example, 60 percent of all exporters with fewer than 19 employees sold to one country market in 2005. Imagine the boost in the bottom line if they could double the number of countries they sell to.

The opportunity for selling into a single region, such as Central America, and taking advantage of free trade agreements, such as the Central America Free Trade Agreement (CAFTA), is substantial. The help available and discussed in this book can quickly expand your thinking—and your sales—from one market to many.

In choosing from among these channels, markets, and countries, what's the best strategy for your business? There's help for that too—from private consultants, from your home state and local U.S. government sources, from the Web, and from this book. And much of the help is free or costs very little. It is easy to access, easy to use.

If what you read so far comes as a surprise—particularly that exporting is relatively easy, even for very small businesses, and that there are scores of local yet worldly folks ready to help you succeed—then you are not alone. The people whom we interviewed for the case studies in this book—like many potential exporters—say that their number one need is for more basic information on how to export.

Surprised? Then you also might be surprised by the old global business assumptions and the new ones replacing them.

This book is mainly written for you, the millions of business owners or their business development gurus who could export or export more. You've asked to have spelled out in plain language how people busy running their businesses can learn what they need to know to grow their sales globally. And here it is: *A Basic Guide to Exporting*.

If you purchased this book or received it from one of our corporate partners, chances are you have already answered for yourself this fundamental question: Why bother?

Exporting can be one of the best ways to grow your business:

- Grow your bottom line.
- Smooth your business cycles.
- Use production capabilities fully.
- Defend your domestic market.
- Increase your competitiveness in all markets.

Exporting is strategic in another way. With the volume of trade growing exponentially and barriers to trade falling, competition in a company's domestic market is intensifying, particularly from foreign competitors. We need to compete in our own backyard while we simultaneously open markets for our products and services in other markets:

- Ninety-five percent of the world's consumers live outside the United States. That is a lot of potential customers to just ignore.
- Foreign competition is increasing domestically. To be truly competitive, companies must consider opening markets abroad.
- Exporting is profitable. In fact, 60 percent of small companies that engage in exporting derive 20 percent of their annual earnings from exports.
- Exporting helps businesses learn how to compete more successfully.

According to a World Bank report, *Global Economic Prospects,* trade in goods and services is likely to more than triple by 2030. Over the same period, the global economy will probably expand from $35 trillion in 2005 to $72 trillion. The number of people considered "middle-class" will triple to 1.2 billion, enabling them to afford international travel, better education, and imported goods from the United States. Exports from the United States, according to the same report, are expected to grow by nearly 10 percent per year for the next several years. Your product or service could be among them.

With this significant projected growth in global trade, fueled in large part by newly affluent consumers in China, India, and other developing economies, the challenge for businesses of all sizes in the United States is how to dip into this incredible revenue torrent. *A Basic Guide to Exporting* aims to help prime your pump.

As global trade grows, companies that engage in it report a shift in income derived from their export sales compared with sales in their domestic markets. A 2002 study of U.S. exporters found that 60 percent of small companies in the survey derived 20 percent of annual earnings from exports, while 44 percent of medium-sized companies did. When asked whether export sales would grow at least 5 percent per year for the next three years, 77 percent of the small firms and 83 percent of the medium-sized firms said they would.

You might reasonably respond by saying, "That's all well and good, but do I have what a person in another country will buy?" As you delve further into this book, you'll read about companies of all sorts that produce an amazing array of products and services and have grown their businesses through exports. Waterless urinals to Japan? Flooded with new orders. Chocolates to the Middle East? No problem. Fiberglass dome houses to India? Business is booming. Pollution eating microbes to Argentina? Can't keep the little critters in stock. Industrial lubricants to Vietnam? The skids are being greased for other markets in Southeast Asia. Franchise concepts in Europe? Everything from furniture moving to senior citizens' companion services.

Even companies that don't make anything are flourishing abroad. These companies make money by providing wholesale and distribution services. And there are thousands of them—all small.

Another answer to "Why bother?" is that exporting adds to the knowledge and skills of everyone in a company who does it. Doing business in a market that's beyond one's borders can have a transformational effect on its practitioners. The experience of forming new relationships, getting up close and personal with another culture, figuring out how to meet the needs of others, and learning how to be inventive in addressing new business challenges not only is personally rewarding; it also leads to improvements in products and makes companies stronger in whatever market they compete.

As one small exporter interviewed for this book put it, "Exporting is easier than we imagined. Exporting opens your horizons to what's going on in the world economy. We need to take that step outside ourselves and develop relationships and open doors. It may start out small. It did for us. But it's growing. We are a better company and better managers. Maybe even better persons. And to me that's what success is all about."

FACT: Exports accounted for nearly 26 percent of U.S. economic growth during the past decade, and they are expected to grow by nearly 10 percent per year for the next several years.

INSIGHT: Exporting has brought growth to many U.S. businesses. It can bring growth to your business too.

FACT: Some small business owners think that exporting is too risky.

INSIGHT: Exporting to some markets, such as Canada, is no more risky than selling in the United States. Different international markets have different levels of risks. Almost any perceived risk can be identified and reduced by using the affordable export assistance now available.

Chapter 2: DEVELOPING AN EXPORT STRATEGY

In This Chapter:

- Is your company ready to export?
- How will exporting affect your company?
- How do you create an export plan?

Determining your Products' Export Potential

There are several ways to evaluate the export potential of your products and services in overseas markets. The most common approach is to examine the domestic sales of your products. If your company is successful in the U.S. market, there is a good chance that it will also sell in markets abroad, at least in those markets where similar needs and conditions exist.

Another way to assess your company's potential in exporting is by examining the unique or important features of your product. If those features are hard to duplicate abroad, then it's likely that your product will be successful overseas. A unique product may have little competition; thus, demand for it may be quite high.

Finally, your product may have export potential even if sales are declining in the U.S. market. Sizable export markets may still exist, especially if the product once did well here but is now losing market share to more technically advanced products. Other countries may not need state-of-the-art technology and may be unable to afford the most sophisticated and expensive products.

FACT: Many companies assume that they can't compete overseas.

INSIGHT: Even if your product or service has no obvious foreign market yet, the world is a big place with many needs and appetites. Remember, price isn't the only selling point. Other factors, such as need, utility, quality, innovation, service, and consumer taste, can make your company competitive.

Assessing Your Company's Export Readiness

As Box 2.1 suggests, export-ready companies possess certain qualities that increase the likelihood that their exporting efforts will be successful. Answering these important questions about how exporting will enhance your company's goals will help determine your company's readiness to export:

- What does your company want to gain from exporting?
- Is exporting consistent with other company goals?
- What demands will exporting place on your company's key resources, management and personnel, production capacity, and financing, and how will these demands be met?
- Are the expected benefits worth the costs, or would company resources be better used for developing new domestic business?

For a more theoretical assessment, it is helpful to examine some of the motivational and organizational factors behind your company's decision to export. Thinking about these factors will help you decide if your company and your product are ready to export.

Motivational factors include the following:

- **Long-term expansion.** Building an exporting plan takes time, so it is important to focus on expanding your business over the long term and not to look for immediate returns.
- **Increased competitiveness.** By selling internationally, your company can gain insights into different ways of doing business.
- **Exploitation of unique technology and expertise.** If your product quality or expertise is superior, you'll have a competitive edge in the international marketplace.
- **Improved return on investment.** Your company should seek multiple benefits from exporting, such as expanded customer networks and exposure to new ideas and technology.
- **Increased capabilities.** You'll develop better products and services, acquire better leadership abilities, and collaborate better with customers and suppliers.

FACT: Many companies never explore the possibility of exporting because they think that they are too small.

INSIGHT: Nearly 97 percent of U.S. exporters are small and medium-sized companies.

Organizational factors include the following:

- **Management commitment.** Total backing from management is the number one determining factor of export success.
- **Funding support.** Management must be willing to allocate sufficient time, enough resources, and an adequate budget for export activities.
- **Personal expertise and commitment.** Having staff members with international experience or having employees learn about your target market's language and culture will help you enter the international marketplace.
- **Product capabilities.** Your company must possess the space and equipment needed to manufacture for the specific countries you are selling to (each of which will have its own product standards and regulations).
- **Company's exporting goals.** Whatever your goal, consider whether the expected benefits outweigh the costs.

Is your product ready to export? To determine export readiness, consider these additional factors:

- **Selling points.** If your product is a success domestically, the next step is to identify why it sells or has sold so well here, keeping in mind that conditions abroad may be somewhere between slightly and significantly different (socially, culturally, economically, politically, and environmentally).
- **Modifications.** You may sell your product without modifications to international markets, as long as it meets the standards and regulations set by the respective countries. Some countries have strict governmental regulations that require special testing, safety, quality, and technical conformity measures.
- **Product licensing.** Some classifications of products require special approval from the U.S.
- Department of Commerce before you export and some of those products require export licenses.
- **Required training.** Products that require training to operate place a greater responsibility on your company and distributor or agent, and you must decide how to support that training.
- **After-sales service.** Products that require considerable after-sales support must be handled by a distributor or agent who is well positioned to provide such a service.
- **Product distinctiveness.** Products that have unique features enjoy a competitive advantage and better reception in foreign markets. Such unique features include patents, superior quality, cutting-edge technology, and adaptability.

FACT: Depending on the target market, it can take months, sometimes even several years, before an exporting company begins to see a return on investment of time and money.

INSIGHT: Written plans provide a clear understanding of your long-term exporting objectives and ensure that management is committed to achieving them.

FACT: Many companies begin export activities haphazardly and are unsuccessful in their early efforts because of poor or no planning, which often leads them to abandon exporting altogether.

INSIGHT: Formulating an export strategy that is based on good information and proper assessment increases the chances that the best options will be chosen, that resources will be used effectively, and that efforts will be carried through to success.

Developing an Export Plan

Once you've decided to sell your products abroad, you'll need to develop an export plan.

A crucial first step in planning is to develop broad consensus among key management personnel on the company's goals, objectives, capabilities, and constraints. In addition, because they will ultimately be responsible for its successful implementation and execution, the personnel involved in the exporting process should agree on all aspects of an export plan.

The purposes of the export plan are (a) to assemble facts, constraints, and goals and (b) to create an action statement that takes all of those elements into account. The plan includes specific objectives, sets forth time schedules for implementation, and marks milestones so that the degree of success can be measured and motivate personnel.

The following 10 questions should ultimately be addressed:

1. Which products are selected for export development, and what modifications, if any, must be made to adapt them for overseas markets?

2. Which countries are targeted for sales development?

3. In each country, what are the basic customer profile, and what marketing and distribution channels should be used to reach customers?

4. What special challenges pertain to each market (for example, competition, cultural differences, and import controls), and what strategy will be used to address them?

5. How will your product's export sales price be determined?

6. What specific operational steps must be taken and when?

7. What will be the time frame for implementing each element of the plan?

8. What personnel and company resources will be dedicated to exporting?

9. What will be the cost in time and money for each element?

10. How will results be evaluated and used to modify the plan?

The first time an export plan is developed, it should be kept simple. It need be only a few pages long because important market data and planning elements may not yet be available.

The initial planning effort itself gradually generates more information and insight. As you learn more about exporting and your company's competitive position, the export plan will become more detailed and complete.

From the start, your plan should be written and viewed as a flexible management tool, not as a static document. Objectives in the plan should be compared with actual results to measure the success of different strategies. Your company should not hesitate to modify the plan and make it more specific as new information and experience are gained.

A detailed plan is recommended for companies that intend to export directly. Companies that choose indirect export methods may use much simpler plans.

Chapter 3: DEVELOPING A MARKETING PLAN

In This Chapter

- **Writing a marketing strategy**
- **Researching foreign markets**

FACT: The world economy grew by an estimated 3.8 percent in 2006 and is expected to continue to grow during the next few years.

INSIGHT: A high rate of economic growth around the world means more opportunities for business. The trick is to pick international markets where growth prospects appear most promising. That's where a solid marketing strategy comes into play.

Many foreign markets differ greatly from markets in the United States. Some differences include climatic and environmental factors, social and cultural factors, local availability of raw materials or product alternatives, lower wage costs, varying amounts of purchasing power, availability of foreign exchange, and government import controls. Once you've decided that your company is able to export and is committed to it, the next step is to develop a marketing plan.

A clear marketing strategy offers six immediate benefits:

1. Written plans readily display strengths and weaknesses.

2. Written plans are not easily forgotten, overlooked, or ignored by those charged with executing them. If deviation from the original plan occurs, it is likely to be the result of a deliberate and thoughtful choice.

3. Written plans are easier to communicate to others and are less likely to be misunderstood.

4. Written plans allocate responsibilities and provide for an evaluation of results.

5. Written plans are helpful when you are seeking financial assistance. They indicate to lenders that you have a serious approach to the export venture.

6. Written plans give management personnel a clear understanding of what will be required of them and help ensure a commitment to exporting.

This last advantage is especially important. Building an international business takes time. It often takes months, sometimes even several years, before an exporting company begins to see a return on its investment of time and money. By committing to the specifics of a written plan, you can make sure that your company will finish what it begins and that the hopes that prompted your export efforts will be fulfilled.

Market Research

To successfully export your product, you should research foreign markets. The purpose is to identify marketing opportunities and constraints abroad, as well as to identify prospective buyers and customers. Market research encompasses all methods that your company may use to determine which foreign markets have the best potential for your products. Results of this research tell you the following:

- The largest markets for your product and the fastest-growing markets
- Market trends and outlook
- Market conditions and practices
- Competing firms and products

Your firm may begin to export without conducting any market research if it receives unsolicited orders from abroad. A good first step is to review your current customer list; if you are engaged in e-commerce, you probably already have customers in foreign countries or have received queries from foreign buyers. These current and prospective foreign customers can be a good barometer for developing an export marketing plan. Although this type of research is valuable, your company may discover even more promising markets by conducting a systematic search.

Primary Market Research

You may research a market by using either primary or secondary data resources. When conducting primary market research, you collect data directly from the foreign marketplace through interviews, surveys, and other direct contact with representatives and potential buyers. Primary market research has the advantage of being tailored to your company's needs and provides answers to specific questions, but the collection of such data on your own is time consuming and expensive and may not be comprehensive. The U.S. Commercial Service can collect primary data for you and help you analyze it. This service costs, on average, several hundred dollars for each market analyzed and does not require you to travel there. The U.S. Commercial Service can also help you find intermediaries with specific market expertise.

Secondary Market Research

When conducting secondary market research, your company collects data from various sources, such as trade statistics for a country or a product. Working with secondary sources is less expensive and helps your company focus its marketing efforts. Although secondary data sources are critical to market research, they do have limitations. The most recent statistics for some countries may be more than a few years old, or the data may be too broad to be of much value to your company.

FACT: Many firms export indirectly, through intermediaries such as export management companies, export trading companies, or other kinds of trading firms.

INSIGHT: If your company does so, it may wish to select markets and conduct market research before selecting the intermediary.

Methods of Market Research

Because of the expense of primary market research, most firms rely on secondary data sources. These three recommendations will help you obtain useful secondary information:

1. Keep abreast of world events that influence the international marketplace, watch for announcements of specific projects, or simply visit likely markets. For example, a thawing of political hostilities often leads to the opening of economic channels between countries. A steep depreciation in the value of the dollar can make your product considerably more competitive.

2. Analyze trade and economic statistics. Trade statistics are generally compiled by product category and by country. Such statistics provide your firm with information concerning shipments of products over specified periods of time. Demographic and general economic statistics, such as population size and makeup, per capita income, and production levels by industry, can be important indicators of the market potential for your company's products.

3. Obtain advice from experts. There are several ways of gathering this advice:

- Contact experts at the U.S. Department of Commerce and other government agencies.
- Attend seminars, workshops, and international trade shows in your industry.
- Hire an international trade and marketing consultant.
- Talk with successful exporters of similar products, including members of District Export Councils in your local area.
- Contact trade and industry associations.

Gathering and evaluating secondary market research may be complex and tedious. However, several publications are available that may simplify the process. The following approach to market research refers to the publications and resources that are described later in this chapter.

A Step-by-Step Approach to Market Research

Your company may find the following approach useful. It involves screening potential markets, assessing the targeted markets, and drawing conclusions.

Screening Potential Markets

STEP 1: OBTAIN EXPORT STATISTICS

Published statistics that indicate product exports to various countries provide a reliable indicator of where U.S. exports are currently being shipped. The U.S. Census Bureau provides these statistics in a published format.

STEP 2: IDENTIFY POTENTIAL MARKETS

First, you should identify 5 to10 large and fast-growing markets for your firm's product. Look at trends over the past three to five years. Has market growth been consistent year to year? Did import growth occur even during periods of economic recession? If not, did growth resume with economic recovery?

Then, take a look at some smaller, fast-emerging markets that may provide ground floor opportunities. If the market is just beginning to open up, there may be fewer competitors than in established markets. To qualify as up-and-coming markets, these countries should have substantially higher growth rates. Libya (which recently opened its economy after years of economic sanctions) and Morocco (which entered into a free trade agreement with the United States in 2005) are good examples of such markets.

Look also at groupings of countries such as those the United States has free trade agreements with in Latin America. Or look at regions within large countries such as western Canada or far eastern Russia. The U.S. Commercial Service has regional services that will help you find buyers in multiple countries in, for example, East Asia. If you're targeting Hong Kong and the Pearl River Delta area, why not stop in nearby Thailand or Singapore?

STEP 3: TARGET THE MOST PROMISING MARKETS

Of the markets you have identified, select three to five of the most statistically promising for further assessment. Consult with a U.S. Commercial Service Export Assistance Center, business associates, freight forwarders, and others to further evaluate targeted markets.

Assessing Targeted Markets

STEP 1: EXAMINE PRODUCT TRENDS

Look not only at company products but also at related products that could influence demand. Calculate overall consumption of the product and the amount accounted for by imports. The U.S. Commercial Service offers market research reports that provide economic background and market trends by country and industry. Demographic information (such as population and age) can be obtained from the Census Bureau and from the United Nations Statistics Division at.

STEP 2: RESEARCH THE COMPETITION

Sources of competition include the domestic industry in each targeted market and competitors from other foreign countries. Look at each competitor's U.S. market share as well as its share in the targeted market.

STEP 3: ANALYZE MARKETING FACTORS

Analyze factors affecting the marketing and use of your product in each market, such as end-user sectors; channels of distribution; cultural idiosyncrasies (for example, does your product's name, when translated into the local language, mean something undesirable?); and business practices. Again, the market research reports and customized market research offered by the U.S. Commercial Service are useful.

STEP 4: IDENTIFY ANY BARRIERS

Foreign barriers to imports can be tariff or non-tariff. U.S. barriers could include export controls. If you make a product that may have dual use (civilian and military), you may be required to have an export license. The U.S. Commercial Service can help you determine whether a license is necessary. Most applications are approved. Call (800) USA-TRADE (800-872-8723) for more information.

STEP 5: IDENTIFY ANY INCENTIVES

The U.S. or foreign government may offer incentives that promote exporting of your particular product or service.

Drawing Conclusions

After analyzing the data, your company may conclude that your marketing resources would be applied more effectively to a few select countries. In general, if your company is new to exporting, then efforts should be directed to fewer than 10 markets. Exporting to a manageable number of countries allows you to focus your resources without jeopardizing your domestic sales efforts. Your company's internal resources should determine what choices you make. The U.S. government, though, has export promotion programs that can assist you with exporting to multiple markets in the same region. The U.S. Commercial Service, for example, has regional export promotion programs in Asia, Europe, the Middle East, and the Americas in addition to country- and industry-specific resources.

FACT: Many small companies could sharply boost exports by entering new markets. In 2005, nearly two-thirds of the small firms that exported posted sales to only one foreign market.

INSIGHT: The U.S. Commercial Service's standardized and customized market research can help you identify additional markets that are appropriate for your products and services.

Sources of Market Research

There are many domestic and international sources of information concerning international markets. This section describes the market research sources that have been mentioned, as well as some additional ones. Because so many research sources exist, your firm may wish to seek advice from your local Export Assistance Center to find the best and most current information.

Research sources range from simple trade statistics, to in-depth market surveys, to firsthand interviews with public- and private-sector experts. Trade statistics indicate total exports or imports by country and by product. They allow you to compare the size of the market for a product in various countries. Some statistics also reflect the U.S. share of the total market in a country in order to gauge the overall competitiveness of U.S. producers. By looking at statistics over several years, you can determine which markets are growing and which are shrinking for your product.

Market surveys provide a narrative description and assessment of particular markets along with relevant statistics. The reports are often based on original research conducted in the countries studied and may include specific information on both buyers and competitors.

One of the best sources of information is personal interviews with private and government officials and experts. A surprisingly large number of people in both the public and private sectors are available to assist you in any aspect of international market research. Either in face-to-face interviews or by telephone, these individuals can provide a wealth of market research information.

Other sources of market research expertise include local chambers of commerce, world trade centers, or clubs and trade associations. Many state governments maintain active export promotion offices. In the federal government, industry and commodity experts are available through the U.S. Departments of Commerce, State, and Agriculture and through the Small Business Administration (SBA).

The following sources are divided into several categories: (a) general information about exporting, (b) statistical and demographic information, (c) export opportunities at development agencies, (d) industry information, and (e) regional and country information.

General Information about Exporting

The following resources are an excellent starting point for obtaining general information.

TRADE INFORMATION CENTER

The Trade Information Center (TIC) of the U.S. Commercial Service is the first stop for companies seeking export assistance from the federal government. TIC trade specialists can:

- Give you information about all government export programs
- Direct you to your local Export Assistance Center for face-to-face export counseling
- Guide you through the export process
- Provide business counseling by country and region on standards and trade regulations, distribution channels, opportunities and best prospects for U.S. companies, tariffs and border taxes, customs procedures, and common commercial difficulties
- Direct you to market research and trade leads
- Provide information on overseas and domestic trade events and activities

Extensive market and regulatory information by region and country is available, including assistance with the North American Free Trade Agreement (NAFTA) certificate of origin and other free trade agreement processes. Call (800) USA-TRADE (800-872-8723) to speak to a TIC specialist.

SMALL BUSINESS ADMINISTRATION EXPORTING TOOLS AND RESOURCES

SBA provides tools and resources to assist small businesses that are considering exporting or those looking to expand into foreign markets.

Statistical and Demographic Information

Current statistical and demographic information is easy to find and available from many sources.

STAT-USA/Internet

This service provides a comprehensive collection of business, economic, and trade information available on the Web. Through this address, you can access daily trade leads and economic news, as well as the latest economic press releases and statistical series from the federal government. For more information on this low-cost service, call (800) STAT-USA (800-782-8872).

USA TRADE ONLINE

For a small subscription fee, you can access This service, offered by STAT-USA in conjunction with the U. S. Census Bureau offers specific, up-to-date export information on more than 18,000 commodities worldwide the latest official statistics on U.S. foreign trade.

EURO TRADE ONLINE

This service, also offered by STAT-USA, provides access to statistics on import and export merchandise trade for each of 25 European countries. Trade data are provided for over 12,000 commodities, using the eight-digit Harmonized System tariff classification structure. These are the official European foreign trade statistics from the European Union's statistical agency, EuroStat.

TRADE STATS EXPRESS

This Web site is a comprehensive source for U.S. export and import data, both current and historical. Maintained by the U.S. Commerce Department's Office of Trade and Industry Information, it contains U.S. trade statistics by country and commodity classifications, state and metropolitan area export data, and trade and industry statistics.

STATISTICAL YEARBOOK

Published by the United Nations, this yearbook is one of the most complete statistical reference books available. It provides international trade information on products, including information on importing countries, which can be useful in assessing import competition. The yearbook contains data on more than 550 commodities for more than 200 countries and territories on economic and social subjects, including population, agriculture, manufacturing, commodity, export-import trade, and many other areas. The book is available only in hard copy; however, the data in the book can be found online in the United Nations Common Database.

WORLD BANK ATLAS AS AND WORLD DEVELOPMENT INDICATORS

Published every two years, the *World Bank Atlas* provides demographics, gross domestic products, and average growth rates for every country. *World Development Indicators* is an annual publication containing more than 800 economic, social, and other indicators for 159 economies, plus basic indicators for another 55 economies.

You can order World Bank publications by mail from The World Bank, P.O. Box 960, Herndon, VA 20172-0960. Purchase World Bank publications by telephone at (800) 645-7247 or on the Web.

WORLD FACT BOOK

Produced annually by the U.S. Central Intelligence Agency (CIA), this publication provides country-by-country data on demographics, the economy, communications, and defense. To purchase the latest print edition, contact the U.S. Government Printing Office Order Desk at *http://bookstore.gpo.gov* or telephone (202) 512-1800.

INTERNATIONAL FINANCIAL STATISTICS

Published by the International Monetary Fund (IMF), *International Financial Statistics* presents statistics on exchange rates, money and banking, production, government finance, interest rates, and other subjects. It is available in hard copy as a monthly subscription, on CD-ROM, or as an online service. Contact the International Monetary Fund, Publication Services, 700 19th St., N.W., Room 12-607, Washington, DC 20431, or telephone (202) 623-7430.

GLOBAL POPULATION PROFILE

This resource is produced by the Census Bureau of the U.S. Department of Commerce. The bureau collects and analyzes worldwide demographic data that can help exporters identify potential markets for their products. Information on each country—total population, fertility, and mortality rates; urban population; growth rate; and life expectancy—is updated every two years. The document also contains detailed demographic profiles of individual countries, including analyses of labor force structure and infant mortality.

Export Opportunities at Development Agencies

International development agencies offer many opportunities for exporters. Here are a few sources to explore.

MULTILATERAL DEVELOPMENT BANKS

Multilateral development banks (MDBs) are institutions that provide financial support and professional advice for economic and social development activities in developing countries. The term *multilateral development bank* typically refers to the World Bank Group or four regional development banks: the African Development Bank, the Asian Development Bank, the European Bank for Reconstruction and Development, and the Inter-American Development Bank. Development projects funded by these banks often offer export opportunities. The U.S. Department of Commerce maintains liaison offices with each of the MDBs in an effort to provide information to U.S. companies on procurements for these projects.

BUDGET JUSTIFICATION TO THE CONGRESS OF THE U.S. AGENCY FOR INTERNATIONAL DEVELOPMENT

Published by the Office of Small and Disadvantaged Business, U.S. Agency for International Development (USAID), the annual *Budget Justification to the Congress* contains individual reports on countries that USAID will provide funds to in the coming year, as well as detailed information on past funding activities in each country. Because the initiatives require U.S. goods and services, these reports give U.S. exporters an early look at upcoming projects. (See Chapter 6 for more details on USAID's programs.) Budget justifications for the current and previous years are available online.

Industry Information

Industry-specific information is important in any exporting venture. Here are a few research avenues.

U.S. DEPARTMENT OF AGRICULTURE, FOREIGN AGRICULTURAL SERVICE

The Foreign Agricultural Service (FAS) serves as the first point of contact for those needing information on foreign markets for agricultural products. The Office of Outreach and Exporter Assistance of the FAS can provide basic export counseling and direct you to the appropriate Department of Agriculture office to answer specific questions on exporting. The staff can provide country- and commodity-specific foreign market information reports, which focus on the best market prospects and contain contact information on distributors and importers.

TEXTILE AND APPAREL DATABASE

Prepared by the U.S. Department of Commerce's Office of Textiles and Apparel, this database provides information on overseas markets and the rules and regulations affecting U.S. exports. The database provides specific country profiles, which include information on marketing and distribution, market-entry requirements, shipment and entry procedures, and trade policy. More general information, such as export procedures, potential buyers and suppliers, current trade issues, and background on textile and apparel trade policy agreements, is also available.

PRIVATE-SECTOR PRODUCT AND INDUSTRY RESOURCES

The U.S. and foreign private sectors publish numerous guides and directories that provide valuable information for your company. For specific references, consult your local Export Assistance Center or the Trade Information Center at (800) USA-TRADE (800-872-8723).

Regional and Country Information

Information on individual countries and regions is widely available. Here are some places you can explore individual markets.

FACT: China is our third-largest export market. U.S. exports to China were up more than 30 percent for 2006, compared with 2005.

INSIGHT: Your company can benefit from this growing market. Visit the China Business Information Center at www.export.gov/china.

CHINA BUSINESS INFORMATION CENTER

The China Business Information Center (BIC) is a comprehensive source of information on China published by federal and state government agencies, associations, and private-sector entities. Companies that are new to the market or are current market participants can use the China BIC to

- Identify sources of U.S. and state government assistance
- Learn how to protect their intellectual property rights
- Monitor China's compliance with its World Trade Organization (WTO) obligations
- Obtain industry-specific market research to evaluate export prospects
- Search for trade leads and tender offers
- Participate in trade events in the United States and China
- Identify sources of trade finance
- Monitor changes in Chinese import regulations
- Identify relevant U.S. export regulations
- Quickly find tips on doing business in China

- Learn about economic and political conditions in China

ASIA NOW

This program brings together the resources of U.S. Commercial Service offices in 14 markets in the Asia-Pacific region and Export Assistance Centers throughout the United States, providing your company with a single point of access to regional trade events, extensive services of the Commercial Service, and research covering Asian markets.

MIDDLE EAST AND NORTH AFRICA BUSINESS INFORMATION CENTER

The Middle East and North Africa Business Information Center (MENABIC) covers information on markets throughout the region: Algeria, Bahrain, Egypt, Iraq, Israel, Jordan, Kuwait, Lebanon, Morocco, Oman, Qatar, Saudi Arabia, Tunisia, the United Arab Emirates, and the West Bank and Gaza. The Web site includes detailed country and industry information, trade leads, lists of trade events both domestically and in MENABIC countries, and information on regulations, licensing, documents, financing, and anything else your company needs to do business in the Middle East and North Africa.

SHOWCASE EUROPE

This program provides U.S. companies easy access to European export markets. The U.S. Commercial Service at U.S. embassies and consulates works with companies to increase exports of U.S. products and services to Europe. You will find trade opportunities, new business partners, market research, and one-on-one assistance for eight key industry sectors, including medical equipment, information technology, and aerospace equipment. The advantages for your company include the following:

- Services at major European trade shows that enable U.S. exhibitors to leverage the event for maximum success
- A systematic approach to counseling in areas such as developing market entry strategies and replicating best practices throughout Europe
- A coordinated approach to market research in an effort to offer U.S. exporters market intelligence that can be more easily replicated across national borders
- Services such as "Quick Take" that provide a quick assessment of your product or service in specific markets

TRADE AMERICAS

The Trade Americas program offers U.S. companies the opportunity to find out more about business opportunities in more than 20 countries throughout the Western Hemisphere. By combining resources across the region, the U.S. Commercial Service helps exporters find sales opportunities in several countries, saving time and money and generating more profits. Trade Americas has a Web site that provides information on existing and proposed free trade agreements throughout the region, market research, best prospects in the region, trade event lists, industry-specific information, business service providers, useful links, and key contacts..

OECD PUBLICATIONS

The chartered mission of the Organization for Economic Cooperation and Development (OECD) is to promote its member countries' policies. These policies have been designed to support economic growth, employment, and a high standard of living and to contribute to sound economic expansion in development and trade. OECD publications focus on a broad range of social and economic issues, concerns, and developments. Country-by-country reports on international market information contain import data useful in assessing import competition.

The OECD also publishes economic development surveys that cover each of the 30 member countries of the OECD, plus some additional countries. Each survey presents a detailed analysis of recent developments in market demand, production, employment, prices, wages, and more. Short-term forecasts and analyses of medium-term problems relevant to economic policies are also provided.

Print copies of OECD publications are available from the OECD Publications and Information Center, 2001 L St., NW, Suite 650, Washington, DC 20036-4922, or telephone (202) 785-6323. You can also order the books on the Web or purchase an online subscription.

MARKET RESEARCH LIBRARY

The U.S. Commercial Service's Market Research Library contains more than 100,000 industry- and country-specific market reports, Web sites, events, and trade directory listings, and it covers more than 120 countries and 110 industry sectors. Reports include Country Commercial Guides, Industry Sector Analyses, Marketing Insights, Multilateral Development Bank Reports, Best Markets, other industry or regional reports, and more

CUSTOMIZED MARKET RESEARCH

These reports make use of the worldwide network of the U.S. Commercial Service to help U.S. exporters evaluate their sales potential in a market; choose the best new markets for their products and services, establish effective marketing and distribution strategies in their target markets, identify the competition, determine which factors are most important to overseas buyers, pinpoint impediments to exporting, and understand many other pieces of critical market intelligence. The reports are customized to your specifications.

Chapter 4: EXPORT ADVICE

In This Chapter

- U.S. Commercial Service assistance
- Other government agency assistance
- Assistance from chambers of commerce

FACT: About 30 percent of non-exporters say they would export if they had information on how to get started, such as best markets, potential buyers, and export procedures.

INSIGHT: The U.S. government is the leading provider of this kind of essential market information.

MAKING THE GOVERNMENT WORK FOR YOU

Now that you've had an opportunity to examine some of the factors involved in an exporting and marketing plan, let's review some key sources of assistance. A lot of help is available to your company at little or no cost and makes the exporting process much easier. This chapter gives a brief overview of the assistance available through federal, state, and local government agencies, as well as in the private sector. Other chapters in this guide provide more information on the specialized services of these organizations and how to use them.

U.S. COMMERCIAL SERVICE EXPORT ASSISTANCE CENTERS

The U.S. Commercial Service of the U.S. Department of Commerce maintains a network of international trade specialists in the United States to help American companies export their products and conduct business abroad. International trade specialists are employed in offices known as Export Assistance Centers in more than 100 cities in the United States and Puerto Rico to assist U.S. exporters, particularly small and medium-sized companies. Export Assistance Centers are known as "one-stop shops" because they combine the trade and marketing expertise and resources of the Commercial Service along with the financial expertise and resources of the Small Business Administration and the Export-Import Bank.

Export Assistance Centers also maximize resources by working closely with state and local governments as well as private partners to offer companies a full range of expertise in international trade, marketing, and finance. International trade specialists will counsel your company on the steps involved in exporting, help you assess the export potential of your products, identify markets, and locate potential overseas partners. They work with their international colleagues in more than 80 countries to provide American companies with turnkey solutions in foreign markets.

Each Export Assistance Center can offer information about the following:

- Services to locate and evaluate overseas buyers and representatives, distributors, resellers, and partners
- International trade opportunities
- Foreign markets for U.S. products and services
- Foreign economic statistics
- Export documentation requirements
- U.S. export licensing requirements and import requirements o f foreign nations
- Export trade finance options
- International trade exhibition participation and certification
- Export seminars and conferences

U.S. COMMERCIAL SERVICE OVERSEAS POSTS

Much of the information about trends and actual trade leads in foreign countries is gathered on site by the officers of the Commercial Service. Those officers have a personal understanding of local market conditions and business practices in the countries in which they work. The Commercial Service officers work in more than 150 offices located in more than 80 countries. They provide a range of services to help companies sell in foreign markets:

- Background information on foreign companies
- Agent-distributor locator services
- Market research
- Business counseling
- Assistance in making appointments with key buyers and government officials
- Representations on behalf of companies adversely affected by trade barriers

You can access those services by contacting your nearest U.S. Export Assistance Center. The centers can also provide assistance with business travel before departure by arranging advance appointments with embassy personnel, market briefings, and other services in the cities you will be visiting.

TRADE INFORMATION CENTER, U.S. COMMERCIAL SERVICE

The Trade Information Center (TIC) is a comprehensive resource for information on all federal government export assistance programs and for information and assistance on exporting to most countries

U.S. TRADE AND DEVELOPMENT AGENCY

Industry and international trade specialists in the U.S. Trade and Development Agency (TDA) work directly with individual firms and manufacturing and service associations to identify trade opportunities and obstacles by product or service, industry sector, and market. TDA analysts participate in trade policy development and negotiations, identify market barriers, and advocate on behalf of U.S. companies. TDA's statistical data and analyses are useful in export development. The TDA staff also develops export marketing programs and obtains industry advice on trade matters. To assist U.S. businesses in their export efforts, TDA's industry and international experts conduct executive trade missions, trade fairs, marketing seminars, and business counseling and provide product literature centers.

FACT: Private consultants are expensive.

INSIGHT: It pays to take full advantage of publicly funded sources of assistance before hiring a consultant. When you do hire the consultant, you will receive greater value because your requirements will be more focused.

EXPORT-IMPORT BANK OF THE UNITED STATES

The Export-Import Bank is committed to supporting small business exporters. In fact, about

85 percent of its transactions support small businesses. The Ex-Im Bank's products include specialized small business financing tools such as working capital guarantee and export credit insurance.

The working capital guarantee and insurance products enable small businesses to increase sales by entering new markets, to expand their borrowing base, and to offer buyers financing while carrying less risk. The Ex-Im Bank's working capital guarantee assumes up to 90 percent of the lender's risk so exporters can access the necessary funds to purchase or produce U.S.-made goods and services for export.

ADVOCACY CENTER, U.S. COMMERCIAL SERVICE

For a U.S. company bidding on a foreign government procurement contract, exporting today can mean more than just selling a good product at a competitive price. It can also mean dealing with foreign governments and complex rules. If you feel that the bidding process is not open and transparent or that it may be tilted in favor of your foreign competition, then you need to contact the Advocacy Center. This center coordinates the actions of 19 U.S. government agencies involved in international trade. Advocacy assistance may involve a visit to a key foreign official by a high-ranking U.S. government official, direct support from U.S. officials stationed overseas, letters to foreign decision-makers, and coordinated action by U.S. government agencies and businesses of all types and sizes.

TRADE COMPLIANCE CENTER, U.S. DEPARTMENT OF COMMERCE

The U.S. Department of Commerce's Trade Compliance Center (TCC) is an integral part of efforts by the U.S. government to ensure foreign compliance with trade agreements. Located within the Market Access and Compliance (MAC) unit of the International Trade Administration, TCC systematically monitors, investigates, and evaluates foreign compliance with multilateral, bilateral, and other international trade agreements and standards of conduct to ensure that U.S. firms and workers receive all the benefits that market-opening initiatives provide.

The TCC website site provides a one-stop shop for American exporters facing market access and agreements compliance problems. The fully searchable database contains the texts of approximately 270 bilateral, regional, and multilateral trade and trade-related agreements, along with detailed market access information for more than 90 major U.S. markets. The online service enables U.S. exporters to file complaints about market access and agreements.

TCC can be reached by phone at (202) 482-1191 or by mail at the U.S. Department of Commerce, Room 3415, 14th St. and Constitution Ave., N.W., Washington, DC 20230.

BUREAU OF INDUSTRY AND SECURITY, U.S. DEPARTMENT OF COMMERCE

The Bureau of Industry and Security (BIS) is responsible for control of exports for reasons of national security, foreign policy, and short supply such as "dual use" items with both military and commercial applications. Assistance with compliance with export controls can be obtained directly from your local BIS district office or from the Outreach and Educational Services Division within the BIS's Office of Exporter Services in Washington, D.C., which you may reach at (202) 482-4811. BIS also has two field offices that specialize in counseling on export controls and regulations; call the Western Regional Office at (949) 660-0144 or the San Jose Office at (408) 291-4212.

MINORITY BUSINESS DEVELOPMENT AGENCY, U.S. DEPARTMENT OF COMMERCE

The Minority Business Development Agency (MBDA) identifies opportunities for U.S. minority business enterprises by promoting their ability to grow and compete in the global economy in selected industries. Through an agreement with the International Trade Administration, MBDA provides information on market and product needs worldwide and identifies ways to access education, finance, and technology to help minority businesses succeed. For example, MBDA and the

International Trade Administration coordinate minority business participation in trade events. And the Minority Business Development Center network helps minority businesses to prepare international marketing plans and promotional materials and to identify financial resources.

For general export information, the field organizations of both MBDA and the International Trade Administration provide information kits and details about local seminars.

WHERE ELSE TO LOOK FOR ASSISTANCE

Small Business Administration

The U.S. Small Business Administration (SBA) and its nationwide network of resource partners can assist you with export counseling, training, and financing. SBA has trade promotion and finance managers located in the U.S. Export Assistance Centers. In addition, you can find out more about exporting through the following:

- **SBA district offices.** The Small Business Administration has district offices in every state and territory that are staffed by specialists who understand SBA programs. These specialists can help small businesses succeed in exporting and put them in touch with other local resources.
- **Small Business Development Centers (SBDCs).** SBDCs provide a full range of export assistance services to small businesses, particularly those new to exporting. They also offer counseling, training, managerial support, and trade-finance assistance. Counseling services are provided at no cost to the small business exporter, but fees are generally charged for export training seminars and other SBDC-sponsored export events.
- **SCORE—Counselors to America's Small Businesses.** Many members of SCORE have practical experience in international trade. They can evaluate your company's export potential and strengthen your domestic operations by identifying financial, managerial, or technical problems. SCORE advisers can also help you develop and implement basic export marketing plans that show where and how to sell your goods abroad. You can find more information at *www.score.org/*.

U.S. Department of Agriculture

The U.S. Department of Agriculture offers exporting assistance through the Office of Outreach and Exporter Assistance (OOEA). A part of the Foreign Agricultural Service (FAS), OOEA serves as the first point of contact for exporters of U.S. food, farm, and forest products. It provides them guidance, referrals, and access to foreign market information and assistance in getting information about export-related programs managed by the U.S. Department of Agriculture and other federal agencies. It also serves as a contact point for minority-owned and small businesses seeking assistance in these areas. OOEA will provide basic export counseling and connect you to the appropriate export program, such as the Market Access Program. Questions regarding any of the programs offered by the Department of Agriculture should be directed to OOEA at (202) 720-7420.

National Center for Standards and Certification Information

The National Center for Standards and Certification Information (NCSCI) provides information about foreign standards and certification systems and requirements. In addition to providing comprehensive information on existing standards and certification requirements, NCSCI began a new service in 2005 known as Notify U.S. This free, Web-based e-mail subscription service offers U.S. citizens, industries, and organizations an opportunity to review and comment on proposed foreign technical regulations that can affect their businesses and their access to international markets. By subscribing to the Notify U.S. service, U.S. entities receive, by e-mail, notifications of drafts or changes to domestic and foreign technical regulations for manufactured products. To register, visit the Notify U.S. Web site.

District Export Councils

Besides the immediate services of its Export Assistance Centers, the U.S. Commercial Service has direct contact with seasoned exporters in all aspects of export trade. The U.S. Export Assistance Centers work closely with 58 District Export Councils (including those in Puerto Rico and the U.S. Virgin Islands) made up of nearly 1,500 business and trade experts who volunteer to help U.S. firms develop solid export strategies.

District Export Councils assist in many of the workshops and seminars on exporting that are arranged by the Export Assistance Centers, and they also sponsor their own. District Export Council members may also provide direct, personal counseling to less experienced exporters by suggesting marketing strategies, trade contacts, and ways to maximize success in overseas markets. You can obtain assistance from District Export Councils through the Export Assistance Centers that they are affiliated with.

State and Local Governments

State, county, and city economic development agencies; departments of commerce or development; and other government entities often provide valuable assistance to exporters. The assistance offered by these groups typically includes the following:

- **Export education.** Helping exporters analyze export potential and introducing them to export techniques and strategies, perhaps in the form of group seminars or individual counseling sessions
- **Trade missions.** Organizing trips abroad to enable exporters to call on potential foreign customers
- **Trade shows.** Organizing and sponsoring exhibitions of state-produced goods and services in overseas markets

Financial Institutions

Many U.S. banks have international departments with specialists who are familiar with specific foreign countries and various types of commodities and transactions. Large banks located in major U.S. cities maintain correspondent relationships with smaller banks throughout the country. And with banks in many foreign countries, they may operate their own overseas branches, providing a direct channel to foreign customers.

International banking specialists are generally well informed about export matters, even in areas that fall outside the usual limits of international banking. Banks frequently provide consultation and guidance free of charge to their clients because they derive income from loans to the exporter and from fees for special services. Many banks also have publications available to help exporters. These materials are often devoted to particular countries and their business practices, and they may be a valuable tool for familiarization with a foreign industry. Finally, large banks frequently conduct seminars and workshops on letters of credit, documentary collections, and other banking subjects of concern to exporters.

Among the many services a commercial bank may perform for its clients are the following:

- Exchange of currencies
- Assistance in financing exports
- Collection of foreign invoices, drafts, letters of credit, and other foreign receivables
- Transfer of funds to other countries
- Letters of introduction and letters of credit for travelers
- Credit information on potential representatives or buyers overseas
- Credit assistance to the exporter's foreign buyers

Export Intermediaries

Export intermediaries range from giant international companies to highly specialized small operations. For a fee, they provide a multitude of services, including performing market research, appointing and managing overseas distributors or commission representatives, exhibiting a client's products at international trade shows, advertising, and shipping and preparing documentation. In short, the intermediary can often take full responsibility for the export end of business, relieving the exporter of all details except filling orders.

Intermediaries may work simultaneously for a number of exporters for a commission, salary, or retainer plus commission. Some intermediaries take title to the goods they handle, buying and selling in their own name. The products of a trading company's various clients are often related, although the items usually are not competitive. One advantage to using an intermediary is that it can immediately make available marketing resources that exporters might take years to develop on their own. Many export intermediaries also finance sales and extend credit, facilitating prompt payment to the exporter.

World Trade Centers, International Trade Clubs, and Local Chambers of Commerce

Local or regional World Trade Centers and international trade clubs are composed of area businesspeople who represent firms engaged in international trade and shipping, banks, forwarders, customs brokers, government agencies, and other service organizations involved in world trade. Such organizations conduct educational programs on international business and organize promotional events to stimulate interest in world trade. There are nearly 300 World Trade Centers or affiliated associations in major trading cities in almost 100 countries. By participating in a local association, a company can receive valuable and timely advice on world markets and opportunities from businesspeople who are already knowledgeable in virtually every facet of international business. Among the advantages of membership are the services, discounts, and contacts from affiliated clubs in foreign countries.

Many local chambers of commerce in the United States provide sophisticated and extensive services for members interested in exporting. Among these services are the following:

- Conducting export seminars, workshops, and roundtable discussions
- Providing certificates of origin
- Developing trade promotion programs, including overseas missions, mailings, and event planning
- Organizing U.S. pavilions at foreign trade shows
- Providing contacts with foreign companies and distributors
- Relaying export sales leads and other opportunities to members
- Organizing transportation routings and shipment consolidations
- Hosting visiting trade missions from other countries
- Conducting international activities at domestic trade shows

Industry and Trade Associations

In addition, some industry and trade associations can supply detailed information on market demand for products in selected countries, or they can refer members to export management companies. Industry trade associations typically collect and maintain files on international trade news and trends affecting their industry or line of business. They often publish articles and newsletters that include government research. National and International trade associations often organize large regional, national, and international trade shows themselves.

FACT:

Fifty-eight percent of small business owners belong to one business organization (e.g., an association), and 42 percent belong to more than one.

INSIGHT:

Business and trade associations have these benefits:

- Inform you about government rules and obligations
- Promote your industry or community
- Provide technical information specific to your industry

American Chambers of Commerce Abroad

A valuable and reliable source of market information in any foreign country is the local chapter of the American Chamber of Commerce (AMCHAM). These local chapters are knowledgeable about local trade opportunities, actual and potential competition, periods of maximum trade activity, and similar considerations.

AMCHAMs usually handle inquiries from any U.S. business. Detailed services are ordinarily provided free of charge for members of affiliated organizations. Some AMCHAM have a set schedule of charges for services rendered to non-members. For contact information on AMCHAMs in major foreign markets, call (800) USA-TRADE (800-872-8723).

International Trade Consultants and Other Advisers

International trade consultants can advise and assist a manufacturer on all aspects of foreign marketing. Trade consultants do not normally deal specifically with one product, although they may advise on product adaptation to a foreign market. They research domestic and foreign regulations and also assess commercial and political risk. They conduct foreign market research and establish contacts with foreign government agencies and other necessary resources, such as advertising companies, product service facilities, and local attorneys.

Consultants in international trade can locate and qualify foreign joint venture partners and can conduct feasibility studies for the sale of manufacturing rights, the location and construction of manufacturing facilities, and the establishment of foreign branches. After sales agreements are completed, trade consultants can also ensure that implementation is smooth and that any problems that arise are dealt with effectively.

Trade consultants usually specialize by subject matter and by global area or country. These consultants can advise on which agents or distributors are likely to be successful, what kinds of promotion are needed, who the competitors are, and how to conduct business with the agents and distributors. They are also knowledgeable about foreign government regulations, contract laws, and taxation. Some firms may be more specialized than others. For example, some may be thoroughly knowledgeable about legal issues and taxation and less knowledgeable about marketing strategies.

Many large accounting firms, law firms, and specialized marketing firms provide international trade consulting services. When selecting a consulting firm, you should pay particular attention to the experience and knowledge of the consultant who is in charge of the project. To find an appropriate firm, seek advice from other exporters and from the other resources listed in this chapter, such as the Export Assistance Centers and local chambers of commerce.

Consultants are of greatest value to a firm that has specific requirements. For that reason, and because private consultants are expensive, it pays to take full advantage of publicly funded sources of assistance before hiring a consultant.

Export Seminars

Besides individual counseling sessions, an effective method of informing local business communities of the various aspects of international trade is through conferences, seminars, and workshops. Each year, Export Assistance Centers participate in approximately 5,000 programs on topics such as export documentation and licensing procedures, country-specific market opportunities, export trading companies, and U.S. trade promotion and trade policy initiatives. The seminars are usually held in conjunction with District Export Councils, local chambers of commerce, state agencies, and other trade organizations. Small Business Administration field offices also co-sponsor export training programs with the Department of Commerce, other federal agencies, and various private-sector international trade organizations.

Chapter 5: METHODS AND CHANNELS

In This Chapter:

- Finding the best approach to exporting for your company
- Separating international from domestic business
- Finding overseas partners, agents, and distributors

The most common methods of exporting are indirect selling and direct selling. In indirect selling, an export intermediary such as an export management company (EMC) or an export trading company (ETC) assumes responsibility for finding overseas buyers, shipping products, and getting paid. In direct selling, the U.S. producer deals directly with a foreign buyer. The paramount consideration in determining whether to market indirectly or directly is the level of resources your company is willing to devote to your international marketing effort. Other factors to consider when deciding whether to market indirectly or directly include the following:

- The size of your firm
- Tolerance for risk
- Resources available to develop the market
- The nature of your products or services
- Previous export experience and expertise
- Business conditions in the selected overseas markets

Approaches to Exporting

The way you choose to export your products can have a significant effect on your export plan and specific marketing strategies. The various approaches to exporting relate to your company's level of involvement in the export process. There are at least four approaches that may be used alone or in combination:

1. Passively filling orders from domestic buyers, who then export the product. These sales are indistinguishable from other domestic sales as far as the original seller is concerned. Another party has decided that the product in question meets foreign demand. That party assumes all the risks and handles all the exporting details, in some cases even without the awareness of the original seller. (Many companies take a stronger interest in exporting when they discover that their product is already being sold overseas.)

2. Seeking out domestic buyers who represent foreign end users or customers. Many U.S. and foreign corporations, general contractors, foreign trading companies, foreign government agencies, foreign distributors, retailers, and others in the United States purchase for export. These buyers constitute a large market for a wide variety of goods and services. In this approach, your company may know that its product is being exported, but the domestic buyer still assumes the risks and handles the details of exporting.

3. Exporting indirectly through intermediaries. With this approach, your company engages the services of an intermediary firm that is capable of finding foreign markets and buyers for your products. EMCs, ETCs, international trade consultants, and other intermediaries can give you access to well-established expertise and trade contacts, but you retain considerable control over the process and can realize some of the other benefits of exporting, such as learning more about foreign competitors, new technologies, and other market opportunities.

4. Exporting directly. This approach is the most ambitious and challenging because your company handles every aspect of the exporting process from market research and planning to foreign distribution and payment collections. A significant commitment of management time and attention is required to achieve good results. However, this approach may also be the best way to achieve maximum profits and long-term growth. With appropriate help and guidance from the U.S. Department of Commerce, state trade offices, freight forwarders, shipping companies, international banks, and others, even small or medium-sized firms can export directly. The exporting process today is easier and has fewer steps than ever before. For those who cannot make that commitment, the services of an EMC, ETC, trade consultant, or other qualified intermediary can be of great value.

The first two approaches represent a substantial proportion of total U.S. exports. They do not, however, involve the firm in the export process. Consequently, this book concentrates on the latter two approaches. If the nature of your company's goals and resources makes an indirect method of exporting the best choice, little further planning may be needed. In such a case, the main task is to find a suitable intermediary firm that can handle most export details. Firms that are new to exporting or are unable to commit staff and funds to more complex export activities may find indirect methods of exporting more appropriate.

However, using an EMC or other intermediary does not exclude the possibility of direct exporting for your firm. For example, your company may try exporting directly to nearby markets such as the Bahamas, Canada, or Mexico, while letting an EMC handle more challenging sales to Egypt or Japan. You may also choose to gradually increase the level of direct exporting once you have gained enough experience and sales volume to justify added investment.

Before making those kinds of decisions, you may want to consult trade specialists such as those at the U.S. Commercial Service. They can be helpful in determining the best approach or mix of approaches for you and your company.

Distribution Considerations

Here are some points to consider when distributing your product:

- Which channels of distribution should your company use to market its products abroad?
- Where should your company produce its products, and how should it distribute them in the foreign market?
- What types of representatives, brokers, wholesalers, dealers, distributors, or end-use customers should you use?
- What are the characteristics and capabilities of the available intermediaries?
- Should you obtain the assistance of an EMC or an ETC?

Your answers from Box 2.2 in Chapter 2 can help you determine whether indirect or direct exporting methods are best for your company.

Indirect Exporting

The principal advantage of indirect exporting for a smaller U.S. company is that an indirect approach provides a way to enter foreign markets without the potential complexities and risks of direct exporting. Several kinds of intermediary firms provide a range of export services, and each type of firm can offer distinct advantages to your company.

Confirming Houses

Confirming houses or buying agents represent foreign firms that want to purchase your products. They seek to obtain the desired items at the lowest possible price and are paid a commission by their foreign clients. In some cases, they may be foreign government agencies or quasi-governmental firms empowered to locate and purchase desired goods. An example is a foreign government purchasing mission.

A good place to find these agents is through foreign government embassies and embassy Web sites or through the U.S. Commercial Service.

Export Management Companies

An export management company can act as the export department for producers of goods and services. It solicits and transacts business in the names of the producers it represents or in its own name for a commission, salary, or retainer plus commission. Some EMCs provide immediate payment for the producer's products by either arranging financing or directly purchasing products for resale. Typically, only larger EMCs can afford to purchase or finance exports.

EMCs usually specialize by product or by foreign market, or sometimes by both. Because of their specialization, the best EMCs know their product s and the markets they serve very well and usually have well-established networks of foreign distributors already in place. This immediate access to foreign markets is one of the principal reasons for using an EMC, because establishing a productive relationship with a foreign representative may be a costly and lengthy process.

One disadvantage of using an EMC is that you may lose control over foreign sales. Most exporters are understandably concerned that their product and company image be well maintained in foreign markets. A way for your company to retain sufficient control in such an arrangement is to carefully select an EMC that can meet your company's needs and maintain close communication with you. For example, your company may ask for regular reports on efforts to market your products and may require approval of certain types of efforts, such as advertising programs or service arrangements. If your company wants to maintain this kind of relationship with an EMC, you should negotiate points of concern before entering an agreement.

Export Trading Companies

An export trading company can facilitate the export of U.S. goods and services. Like an EMC, an ETC can either act as the export department for producers or take title to the product. A special kind of ETC is a group organized and operated by producers. These ETCs can be organized along multiple- or single-industry lines and can a lso represent producers of competing products.

Exporters may consider applying for an Export Trade Certificate of Review under the Export Trading Company Act of 1982. A certificate of review provides limited antitrust immunity for specified export activities.

Export Agents, Merchants, or Remarketers

Export agents, merchants, or remarketers purchase products directly from the manufacturer, packing and labeling the products according to their own specifications. They then sell these products overseas through their contacts in their own names and assume all risks.

In transactions with export agents, merchants, or remarketers, your firm relinquishes control over the marketing and promotion of your product. This situation could have an adverse effect on future sales abroad if your product is underpriced or incorrectly positioned in the market or if after-sales service is neglected. However, the effort required by the manufacturer to market the product overseas is very small and may lead to sales that otherwise would take a great deal of effort to obtain.

Piggyback Marketing

Piggyback marketing is an arrangement in which one manufacturer or service firm distributes a second firm's product or service. The most common piggybacking situation occurs when a U.S. company has a contract with an overseas buyer to provide a wide range of products or services.

Often, the first company does not produce all the products that it is under contract to provide, and it turns to other U.S. companies to provide the remaining products. The second U.S. company then piggybacks its products onto the international market, generally without incurring the marketing and distribution costs associated with exporting. Successful arrangements usually require that the product lines be complementary and appeal to the same customers.

Direct Exporting

The advantages of direct exporting for your company include more control over the export process, potentially higher profits, and a closer relationship to the overseas buyer and marketplace, as well as the opportunity to learn what you can do to boost overall competitiveness. However, those advantages come at a price; your company needs to devote more time, personnel, and resources to direct exporting than it would to indirect exporting.

If your company chooses to export directly to foreign markets, it usually will make internal organizational changes to support more complex functions. As a direct exporter, you'll normally select the markets you wish to penetrate, choose the best channels of distribution for each market, and then make specific connections with overseas buyers in order to sell your product.

Getting Organized for Exporting

A company new to exporting generally treats its export sales no differently from its domestic sales, using existing personnel and organizational structures. As international sales and inquiries increase, your company may choose to separate the management of its exports from that of its domestic sales.

The advantages of separating international from domestic business include the centralization of specialized skills needed to deal with international markets and the benefits of a focused marketing effort that is more likely to increase export sales. A possible disadvantage is that segmentation might be a less efficient use of company resources.

Your company can separate international from domestic business at different levels in the organization. For example, when you first begin to export, you may create an export department with a full- or part-time manager who reports to the head of domestic sales and marketing. At a later stage, your company may choose to increase the autonomy of the export department to the point of creating an international division that reports directly to the president. Many smaller companies absorb export sales into existing functions; such an arrangement works effectively until export sales increase significantly.

Regardless of how your company organizes its exporting efforts, the key is to facilitate the marketer's job. Good marketing skills can help your firm operate in an unfamiliar market. Experience has shown that a company's success in foreign markets depends less on the unique attributes of its products than on its marketing methods.

Once your company is organized to handle exporting, a proper channel of distribution needs to be carefully chosen for each market. These channels include sales representatives, agents, distributors, retailers, and end users.

Sales Representatives

An overseas sales representative is the equivalent of a manufacturer's representative in the United States. The representative uses your company's product literature and samples to present the product to potential buyers. Ordinarily, a representative handles many complementary lines that do not conflict. The sales representative usually works for a commission, assumes no risk or responsibility, and is under contract for a definite period of time (renewable by mutual agreement). The contract defines territory, terms of sale, method of compensation, reasons and procedures for terminating the agreement, and other details. The sales representative may operate on either an exclusive or a non-exclusive basis.

Agents or Representatives

The widely misunderstood term agent means a representative who normally has authority—perhaps even a power of attorney—to make commitments on behalf of the firm that he or she represents. Firms in the United States and other developed countries have stopped using that term because agent can imply a power of attorney. They rely instead on the term representative. It is important that the contract state whether the representative or agent has the legal authority to obligate your firm.

Distributors

The foreign distributor is a merchant who purchases goods from a U.S. exporter (often at a discount) and resells them for a profit. The foreign distributor generally provides support and service for the product, relieving the U.S. exporter of those responsibilities. The distributor usually carries an inventory of products and a sufficient supply of spare parts and also maintains adequate facilities and personnel for normal servicing operations. Distributors typically handle a range of non-competing, complementary products. End users do not usually buy from a distributor; they buy from retailers or dealers.

The terms and length of association between your company and the foreign distributor are established by contract. Some U.S. companies prefer to begin with a relatively short trial period and then extend the contract if the relationship proves satisfactory to both parties. The U.S. Commercial Service can help you identify and select distributors and can provide general advice on structuring agreements.

Foreign Retailers

You may also sell directly to foreign retailers, although in such transactions products are generally limited to consumer lines. The growth of major retail chains in markets such as Canada and Japan has created new opportunities for this type of direct sale. The approach relies mainly on traveling sales representatives who directly contact foreign retailers, although results might also be achieved by mailing catalogs, brochures, or other literature.

The direct mail approach has the benefits of eliminating commissions, reducing travel expenses, and reaching a broader audience. For optimal results, a company that uses direct mail to reach foreign retailers should support it with other marketing activities.

American manufacturers with ties to major domestic retailers may also be able to use them to sell abroad. Many large American retailers maintain overseas buying offices and use those offices to sell abroad when practical.

Direct Sales to End Users

You may sell your products or services directly to end users in foreign countries. The buyers may be foreign government institutions or they may be businesses. The buyers can be identified at trade shows, through international publications, or by the overseas posts of the U.S. Commercial Service.

You should be aware that if a product is sold in such a direct fashion, your company is responsible for shipping, payment collection, and product servicing unless other arrangements are made. If the cost of providing these services is not built into the export price, you could have a smaller profit than you had anticipated.

If you choose to use foreign representatives, you can meet them during overseas business trips, at domestic or international trade shows, or through Web sites such as the U.S. Department of Commerce's at www.buyusa.gov/matchmaking. A comprehensive list of upcoming trade shows can be found at www.export.gov/tradeevents. There are other effective methods that you can use without leaving the United States, including e-commerce platforms. Ultimately, you may need to travel abroad to identify, evaluate, and sign up overseas representatives; however, you can save time by first conducting background research in the country you're targeting. The Commercial Service can provide the market research you need and introduce you to buyers in more than 80 countries.

Contacting and Evaluating Foreign Representatives

Once your company has identified a number of potential representatives or distributors in the selected market, you should write, e-mail, or fax each one directly. Just as your firm is seeking information on the foreign representative, the representative is interested in corporate and product information on your firm. The prospective representative may want more information than your company normally provides to a casual buyer. Your firm should provide full information on its history, resources, personnel, product line, previous export activity (if any), and all other relevant matters. Your firm may wish to include a photograph or two of plant facilities and products—and even product samples when practical. You may also want to consider inviting the foreign representative to visit your company's operations. Whenever the danger of intellectual property theft is significant, you should guard against sending product samples that could be easily copied. (For more information on correspondence with foreign firms, see Chapter 17.)

Your firm should investigate potential representatives or distributors carefully before entering into an agreement with them. You also need to know the following information about the representative or distributor:

- Current status and history, including background on principal officers

- Methods of introducing new products into the sales territory

- Trade and bank references

- Data on whether your firm's special requirements can be met

You should also ask for the prospective representative or distributor's assessment of the in-country market potential for your firm's products. Such information is useful in gauging how much the representative knows about your industry; it provides valuable market research as well.

Your company may obtain much of this information from business associates who work with foreign representatives. However, you should not hesitate to ask potential representatives or distributors detailed and specific questions. Suppliers have the right to explore the qualifications of those who propose to represent them overseas. Well-qualified representatives will gladly answer questions that help distinguish them from less qualified competitors. Your company should also consider other private-sector and U.S. government sources for credit checks of potential business partners.

In addition, your company may wish to obtain at least two supporting business and credit reports to ensure that the distributor or representative is reputable. By using a second credit report from a different source, you may gain new or more complete information. Reports from a number of companies are available from commercial firms and from the Commercial Service's International Company Profiles. Commercial firms and banks are also sources of credit information on overseas representatives. They can provide information directly or from their correspondent banks or branches overseas. Directories of international companies may also provide credit information on foreign firms.

Once your company has prequalified some foreign representatives, you may wish to travel to the foreign country to observe the size, condition, and location of their offices and warehouses. In addition, your company should meet each sales force and try to assess its strength in the marketplace. If traveling to each distributor or representative is difficult, you may decide to meet each of them at U.S. or worldwide trade shows. The Commercial Service can arrange the meetings; it also offers videoconferencing, which can, in many instances, replace the need to travel.

Negotiating an Agreement with a Foreign Representative

When your company has found a prospective representative that meets its requirements, the next step is to negotiate a foreign sales agreement. Export Assistance Centers provide advice to firms contemplating that step.

Most representatives are interested in your company's pricing structure and product profit potential. They are also concerned with the terms of payment; product regulation; competitors and their market shares; the amount of support provided by your firm, such as sales aids, promotional material, and advertising; training for the sales and service staff; and your company's ability to deliver on schedule.

The agreement may contain provisions that specify the actions of the foreign representative, including the following:

- Not having business dealings with competing firms (because of antitrust laws, this provision may cause problems in some European countries)
- Not revealing any confidential information in a way that would prove injurious, detrimental, or competitive to your firm
- Not entering into agreements with other parties that would be binding to your firm
- Referring all inquiries received from outside the designated sales territory to your firm for action

To ensure a conscientious sales effort from the foreign representative, the agreement should include a requirement that the representative apply the utmost skill and ability to the sale of the product for the compensation named in the contract. It may be appropriate to include performance requirements, such as a minimum sales volume and an expected rate of increase.

In drafting the agreement, you must pay special attention to safeguarding your company's interests in case the representative proves less than satisfactory. (See Chapter 10 for recommendations on specifying terms of law and arbitration.) It is vital to include an escape clause in the agreement that allows you to end the relationship safely and cleanly if the representative does not fulfill expectations. Some contracts specify that either party may terminate the agreement with written advance notice of 30, 60, or 90 days. The contract may also spell out exactly what constitutes "just cause" for ending the agreement (for example, failure to meet specified performance levels). Other contracts specify a certain term for the agreement (usually one year) but arrange for automatic annual renewal unless either party gives written notice of its intention not to renew.

In all cases, escape clauses and other provisions to safeguard your company may be limited by the laws of the country in which the representative is located. For this reason, you should learn as much as you can about the legal requirements of the representative's country and obtain qualified legal counsel in preparing the contract. These are some of the legal questions to consider:

- How far in advance must the representative be notified of your intention to terminate the agreement? Three months satisfy the requirements of many countries, but a registered letter may be needed to establish when the notice was served.
- What is "just cause" for terminating a representative? Specifying causes for termination in the written contract usually strengthens your position.

- Which country's laws (or which international conventions) govern a contract dispute? Laws in the representative's country may forbid the representative company from waiving its nation's legal jurisdiction.
- What compensation is due to the representative on dismissal? Depending on the length of the relationship, the added value of the market that the representative created for you, and whether termination is for just cause as defined by the foreign country, you may be required to compensate the representative for losses.
- What must the representative give up if dismissed? The contract should specify the return of property, including patents, trademarks, name registrations, and customer records.
- Should the representative be referred to as an agent? In some countries, the word agent implies power of attorney. The contract needs to specify whether the representative is a legal agent with power of attorney.
- In what language should the contract be drafted? In most cases, the contract should be in both English and the official language of the foreign country. Foreign representatives often request exclusivity for marketing in a country or region. It is recommended that you not grant exclusivity until the foreign representative has proven his or her capabilities or that it be granted for a limited, defined period of time, such as one year, with the possibility of renewal. The territory covered by exclusivity may also need to be defined, although some countries' laws may prohibit that type of limitation.

The agreement with the foreign representative should define what laws apply to the agreement. Even if you choose U.S. law or that of a third country, the laws of the representative's country may take precedence. Many suppliers define the United Nations Convention on Contracts for the International Sale of Goods (CISG, or the Vienna Convention) as the source of resolution for contract disputes, or they defer to a ruling by the International Court of Arbitration of the International Chamber of Commerce.

Chapter 6: FINDING QUALIFIED BUYERS

In This Chapter

- U.S. Commercial Service programs to help you find buyers
- Department of Commerce agencies to assist you
- State and local government assistance

By now, your company has identified its most promising markets and devised a strategy to enter those markets. As discussed earlier, your company may sell directly to a customer or may use the assistance of an in-country representative (agents or distributors) to reach the end user. This chapter describes some of the sources that can help you find buyers, evaluate trade shows and missions, and generate sales.

U.S. DEPARTMENT OF COMMERCE WORLDWIDE BUYER FINDING PROGRAMS

The U.S. Department of Commerce can help exporters identify and qualify leads for potential buyers, distributors, joint venture partners, and licensees from both private and public sources. Along with its experts in various products, countries, and programs, the U.S. Department of Commerce has an extensive network of commercial officers posted in countries that represent 95 percent of the market for U.S. products.

Programs available through the U.S. Department of Commerce, including those of the U.S. Commercial Service, are listed in this section. Exporters should contact the nearest Export Assistance Center for more information or call the Trade Information Center at (800) USA-TRADE (800-872-8723).

BuyUSA.gov Matchmaking

BuyUSA.gov Matchmaking is a convenient online program of the U.S. Commercial Service that matches U.S. exporters with buyers and importers in overseas markets. On the basis of the profiles that companies send to BuyUSA.gov, U.S. exporters receive the information that they need to contact potential importers in the overseas markets they select. There's no need to search a database or return to check for new importers; when an importer registers with a profile that matches your export objectives, BuyUSA.gov Matchmaking will automatically notify you. Whether you contact the potential importers is up to you, so you won't receive unwanted contacts by registering for the program.

This program is available to current clients of the U.S. Commercial Service with U.S.-made ready-to-export products or services. If your company is not a current client of the U.S. Commercial Service but you are otherwise qualified for this program, find your nearest U.S. Export Assistance Center and make an appointment with a trade specialist.

Commercial News USA

Commercial News USA (CNUSA) is the official U.S. Department of Commerce showcase for American-made products and services. It provides worldwide exposure for U.S. products and services through an illustrated catalog-magazine and through electronic bulletin boards. CNUSA is designed to help U.S. companies promote products and services to buyers in more than 145 countries. Each issue of the free bimonthly catalog-magazine reaches an estimated 400,000 readers worldwide. CNUSA is mailed directly to qualified recipients and is also distributed by Commercial Service personnel at U.S. embassies and consulates throughout the world.

CNUSA can help your company make sales. Its features include the following:

- **Direct response**. New customers around the world will read about your product or service and will receive information that enables them to contact you directly. Address-coded trade leads make it easy to track results.

- **Built-in credibility**. Distributed by U.S. Commercial Service officials at embassies and consulates, CNUSA enjoys exceptional credibility.

- **Follow-up support**. The U.S. Department of Commerce offers free individual export counseling at any of the Export Assistance Centers across the country.

Featured U.S. Exporters

Featured U.S. Exporters (FUSE) is a directory of U.S. products presented on the Web sites of many U.S. Commercial Service offices around the world. It gives your company an opportunity to target markets in specific countries in the local language of business. This service is offered free of charge to qualified U.S. exporters seeking trade leads or representation in certain markets.

Customized Market Research

Customized market research reports use the Commercial Service's worldwide network to help U.S. exporters evaluate their sales potential in a market, choose the best new markets for their products and services, establish effective marketing and distribution strategies in their target markets, identify the competition, determine which factors are most important to overseas buyers, pinpoint impediments to exporting, and understand many other pieces of critical market intelligence. These customized reports will be built to your specifications.

Gold Key Matching Service

The Gold Key Matching Service is a customized buyer-finding solution offered by the Commercial Service in key export markets around the world. The service includes orientation briefings; market research; appointments with potential partners; interpreter services for meetings; and assistance in closing the deal, shipping the goods, and getting paid. To request a Gold Key Matching Service, contact your local Export Assistance Center.

International Company Profiles

An International Company Profile (ICP) is a background report on a specific foreign firm that is prepared by commercial officers of the United States Commercial Service at American embassies and consulates. These reports include the following:

- Information on the firm
- Year established
- Relative size
- Number of employees
- General reputation
- Territory covered
- Language capabilities
- Product lines handled
- Principal owners
- Financial references
- Trade references

Each ICP also contains a general narrative report by the U.S. Commercial Service officer who conducted the investigation concerning the reliability of the foreign firm.

The ICP service is offered in countries that lack adequate private-sector providers of credit and background information on local companies. Credit reports on foreign companies are available from many private-sector sources, including (in the United States) Dun and Bradstreet and Graydon International. For help in identifying private-sector sources of credit reports, contact your nearest Export Assistance Center International Partner Search

With the U.S. Commercial Service's International Partner Search, teams of experts in more than 80 countries work to find you the most suitable strategic partners. You provide your marketing materials and background on your company. The Commercial Service uses its strong network of international contacts to interview potential partners and to provide you with a list of up to five prescreened companies. By working only with prescreened firms that are interested in buying or selling your products and services, you save valuable time and money.

The International Partner Search allows you to obtain high-quality market information in 15 days. The search yields information on each potential partner's size, sales, years in business, and number of employees, as well as a statement from each potential partner on the marketability of your product or service. You will also receive complete contact information on key individuals among the potential partners who are interested in your company. To obtain more information or to order an International Partner Search, contact your local Export Assistance Center.

DEPARTMENT OF COMMERCE TRADE EVENT PROGRAMS

Some products, because of their nature, are difficult to sell unless the potential buyer has an opportunity to examine them in person. Sales letters and brochures can be helpful, but an actual presentation of products in the export market may prove more beneficial. One way for your company to actually present its products to an overseas market is by participating in trade events such as trade shows, fairs, trade missions, matchmaker delegations, and catalog exhibitions.

Trade fairs are "shop windows" where thousands of firms from many countries display their goods and services. They serve as a marketplace where buyers and sellers can meet with mutual convenience. Some fairs, especially in Europe, have a history that goes back centuries. Also, it is often easier for buyers from certain regions of the world to gather in Europe than the United States.

Attending trade fairs involves a great deal of planning. The potential exhibitor must take into account the following logistic considerations:

- Choosing the proper fair out of the hundreds that are held e very year
- Obtaining space at the fair, along with designing and constructing the exhibit
- Shipping products to the show, along with unpacking and setting up
- Providing proper hospitality, such as refreshments, along with maintaining the exhibit
- Being able to separate serious business prospects from browsers
- Breaking down, packing, and shipping the exhibit home at the conclusion of the fair

A trade magazine or association can often provide information on major shows. Whether privately run or government sponsored, many trade shows have a U.S. pavilion that is dedicated to participating U.S. businesses. For additional guidance, contact your local Export Assistance Center or visit www.export.gov/tradeevents. You can find a complete list of trade events online, and you can search by country, state, industry, or date.

Examples of trade shows are Medtrade, which takes place annually and is geared toward the health care services sector, and the Automotive Aftermarket Industry Week, which is also held annually and is attended by companies in various parts of the automotive industry.

International Buyer Program

The International Buyer Program (IBP) supports major domestic trade shows featuring products and services of U.S. industries with high export potential. Commercial Service officers recruit prospective foreign buyers to attend selected trade shows. The shows are extensively publicized in targeted markets through embassy and regional commercial newsletters, catalog-magazines, foreign trade associations, chambers of commerce, travel agents, government agencies, corporations, import agents, and equipment distributors.

As a U.S. exhibitor at an IBP event, you will receive many valuable free benefits, including the following:

- Opportunities to meet with prospective foreign buyers, representatives, and distributors from all over the world who have been recruited by U.S. Commercial Service specialists in more than 150 cities overseas
- Worldwide promotion of your products and services through the Export Interest Directory, which is published by the show organizers and distributed to all international visitors attending the show
- Access to hundreds of current international trade leads in your industry

- Hands-on export counseling, marketing analysis, and matchmaking services by country and industry experts from the U.S. Commercial Service

- Use of an on-site international business center, where your company can meet privately with prospective international buyers, sales representatives, and business partners and can obtain assistance from experienced U.S. Commercial Service staff members

Each year, the Commercial Service selects and promotes more than 30 trade shows representing leading industrial sectors, including information technology, environmental products and services, medical equipment and supplies, food processing and services, packaging, building and construction products, sporting goods, and consumer products.

Trade Fair Certification Program

The U.S. Department of Commerce Trade Fair Certification Program is a partnership arrangement between private-sector show organizers and the International Trade Administration to assist and encourage U.S. firms to promote their products at appropriate trade fairs abroad. Certification of a U.S. organizer signals to exhibitors, visitors, and the government of the host country that the event is an excellent marketing opportunity and that participants will receive the support of the U.S. government. Certified organizers are authorized to recruit and manage a U.S. pavilion at the show. They are especially focused on attracting small and medium-sized U.S. firms that are new to the market. Certified organizers can help with all aspects of freight forwarding, customs clearance, exhibit design, and on-site services.

Certified organizers receive government assistance, such as the following:

- Designation as the official U.S. pavilion

- Authorized use of an official Commercial Service certification logo

- On-site support and counseling for U.S. exhibitors from the U.S. embassy commercial staff

- Local market information and contact lists

- Press releases and other promotion actions

- Advertising and marketing assistance from Commerce Department Export Assistance Centers

- Support letters from the secretary of commerce and the president of the United States when appropriate

- Exhibitor briefings
- Opening ceremonies, ribbon-cuttings, and dignitary liaison

Trade Missions

The U.S. Department of Commerce organizes or supports numerous trade missions each year. The missions involve travel to foreign countries by U.S. companies and Commerce Department employees. Participants meet face to face with prescreened international businesspeople in the market they travel to. Trade missions save U.S. companies time and money by allowing them to maximize contact with qualified distributors, sales representatives, or partners. U.S. Commercial Service missions are industry specific and target two to four countries per trip. Commercial Service specialists abroad will prescreen contacts, arrange business appointments, and coordinate logistics in advance. This preparatory effort is followed up by a one-week trip by the U.S. company to personally meet with the new prospects.

International Catalog Exhibition Program

The U.S. Commercial Service's International Catalog Exhibition Program offers U.S. companies a convenient, affordable way to stimulate interest in their products and services while never leaving the office. Commercial Service trade specialists located in international markets will translate the company profile into the local language, display the company's marketing materials, collect sales leads from interested local buyers, and then assist the U.S. company as it follows up with the local contacts. There are three types of catalog events:

- Multistate catalog exhibitions target four or more promising international markets, promote U.S. exports in 20 or more high-demand product and service sectors, and leverage the partnership between the Department of Commerce and state economic development agencies.
- American Product Literature Centers target a single promising international market, focus on a single industry sector, and typically take place at a leading industry trade show.
- U.S. embassy and consulate-sponsored catalog exhibits target a single promising international market and are managed by a U.S. embassy or consulate.

For all three types of catalog events, the U.S. Commercial Service will coordinate support from local chambers of commerce, industry associations, and other trade groups; provide trade leads generated by each exhibition; and help capitalize on leads by providing any needed export assistance.

U.S. DEPARTMENT OF AGRICULTURE, FOREIGN AGRICULTURAL SERVICE

Through a network of counselors, attachés, trade officers, commodity analysts, and marketing specialists, the Department of Agriculture's Foreign Agricultural Service (FAS) can help arrange contacts overseas and provide marketing assistance for companies that export agricultural commodities. Extensive information on the FAS is also available on the Internet. Visit the Department of Agriculture FAS Web site.

U.S. AGENCY FOR INTERNATIONAL DEVELOPMENT

The U.S. Agency for International Development (USAID) administers programs that offer export opportunities for U.S. suppliers of professional technical assistance services and commodities. Opportunities to export commodities are available through the commodity import programs that USAID operates in select USAID-recipient countries and through USAID's direct procurement of commodities. In addition, USAID funds may be available in certain recipient countries to finance developmentally sound projects involving U.S. capital goods and services. For exporters traveling to developing countries where a USAID program is in place, information is available on funds, projects under consideration, and contacts. Talk to someone at the nearest Export Assistance Center or call (800) USAID-4U (800-872-4348).

The U.S. Trade and Development Agency (TDA) assists in the creation of jobs for Americans by helping U.S. companies pursue overseas business opportunities. Through the funding of feasibility studies, orientation visits, specialized training grants, business workshops, and various forms of technical assistance, TDA helps American businesses compete for infrastructure and industrial projects in emerging markets.

TDA's mission is to help companies get in on the ground floor of export opportunities and to make them competitive with heavily subsidized foreign companies. Because of its focused mission, TDA considers only infrastructure and industrial projects that have the potential to mature into significant export opportunities for American companies and to create jobs in the United States. Projects are typically in the areas of agriculture, energy and power, health care, manufacturing, mining and minerals development, telecommunications, transportation, and environmental services.

To be considered for TDA funding, projects

- Must face strong competition from foreign companies that receive subsidies and other support from their governments

- Must be a development priority of the country where the project is located and have the endorsement of the U.S. embassy in that nation

- Must represent an opportunity for sales of U.S. goods and services that is many times greater than the cost of TDA assistance
- Must be likely to receive implementation financing and have a procurement process open to U.S. firms

STATE AND LOCAL GOVERNMENT ASSISTANCE

Most states can provide an array of services to exporters. Many states maintain international offices in major markets; the most common locations are in Western Europe and Japan. Working closely with the commercial sections of U.S. embassies in those countries, state foreign offices can assist exporters in making contacts in foreign markets, providing such services as the following:

- Specific trade leads with foreign buyers
- Assistance for trade missions, such as itinerary planning, appointment scheduling, travel, and accommodations
- Promotional activities for goods or services, including representing the state at trade shows
- Help in qualifying potential buyers, agents, or distributors

In addition, some international offices of state development organizations help set up and promote foreign buyer missions to the United States, which can be effective avenues of exporting with little effort. Attracting foreign investment and developing tourism are also very important activities of state foreign offices. More and more cities and counties are providing these same services.

PROMOTION IN PUBLICATIONS AND OTHER MEDIA

A large and varied assortment of magazines covering international markets is available to you through U.S. publishers. They range from specialized international magazines relating to individual industries, such as construction, beverages, and textiles, to worldwide industrial magazines covering many industries. Many consumer publications produced by U.S.-based publishers are also available. Several are produced in national-language editions (e.g., Spanish for Latin America), and some offer "regional buys" for specific export markets of the world. In addition, several business directories published in the United States list foreign representatives geographically or by industry specialization.

Publishers frequently supply potential exporters with helpful market information, make specific recommendations for selling in the markets they cover, help advertisers locate sales representation, and render other services to aid international advertisers.

Many of these magazines and directories are available at libraries, Export Assistance Centers, or the U.S. Department of Commerce's reference room in Washington, D.C. State departments of commerce, trade associations, business libraries, and major universities may also provide such publications.

FACT: Most U.S. exporters simply take orders from abroad rather than vigorously marketing their products or services.

INSIGHT: U.S. government agencies, particularly the U.S. Commercial Service, can help you strategically increase your international sales by indentifying and qualifying leads for potential buyers, distributors, and other partners.

FACT: According to the World Health Organization, diarrhea causes 1.6 million deaths every year—the vast majority among children under five years. Those deaths are related to unsafe water, sanitation, and hygiene. More than a billion people lack access to a clean water source.

INSIGHT: By building infrastructure in the developing world, U.S. companies are improving the quality of life of millions of people and are saving lives.

Chapter 7: USING TECHNOLOGY LICENSING AND JOINT VENTURES

In This Chapter

- **Methods of obtaining foreign trade income**
- **Advantages and disadvantages of technology licensing and joint ventures**

You should consider two alternative ways of obtaining international sales income: technology licensing and joint ventures. Although not necessarily the most profitable forms of exporting, they do offer certain advantages, particularly for small and medium-sized businesses.

TECHNOLOGY LICENSING

Technology licensing is a contractual arrangement in which the licenser's patents, trademarks, service marks, copyrights, trade secrets, or other intellectual property may be sold or made available to a licensee for compensation that is negotiated in advance between the parties. This compensation may be a lump-sum royalty, a running royalty (royalty that is based on volume of production), or a combination of both. U.S. companies frequently license their technology to foreign companies that then use it to manufacture and sell products in a country or group of countries defined in the licensing agreement.

A technology licensing agreement usually enables your firm to enter a foreign market quickly, and it poses fewer financial and legal risks than owning and operating a foreign manufacturing facility or participating in an overseas joint venture. Licensing also permits U.S. firms to overcome many of the tariff and non-tariff barriers that frequently hamper the export of U.S.-manufactured products. For these reasons, licensing can be a particularly attractive method of "exporting" for small companies or companies with little international trade experience, even though small and large firms profitably use this technique. Technology licensing may also be used to acquire foreign technology through cross-licensing agreements or grant back clauses that award rights to improved technology developed by a licensee. Seek legal advice to determine liability where licensing is involved.

Technology licensing is not limited to the manufacturing sector. Franchising is also an important form of technology licensing used by many service industries. In franchising, the franchiser (licenser) permits the franchisee (licensee) to use its trademark or service mark in a contractually specified manner for the marketing of goods or services. The franchiser usually continues to support the operation of the franchisee's business by providing advertising, accounting, training, and related services. In many instances, the franchiser also supplies products needed by the franchisee.

Franchising is not the exclusive domain of well-known brands. Scores of new franchising concepts are converted into profitable businesses every year, and the majorities are created in the United States. Among recent franchising concepts that have gone global are personal fitness, flowers and candy, and elder care. Many of the franchises are being created especially for entrepreneurs in developing countries and feature relatively affordable license fees and other inputs. Attending the International Franchise Association convention and trade fair is a good way to learn about trends and new franchising concepts.

As a form of "exporting," technology licensing has certain potential drawbacks. One negative aspect of licensing is that your control over the technology is weakened because it has been transferred to an unaffiliated firm. Additionally, licensing usually produces fewer profits for your company than exporting actual goods or services. In certain developing countries, there also may be problems in adequately protecting the licensed technology from unauthorized use by third parties.

You should make sure to register your patents and trademarks in this country. Copyright is recognized globally, but your patents and trademarks are territorial, meaning that rights are defined and interpreted differently. For this reason, you need to file your patents and trademarks with each country you intend to do business in. An exception is the European Union (EU), because its laws apply to all members. The Patent Cooperative Treaty and the Madrid Protocol allow you to register your patents and trademarks in your home country and apply for protection in the EU as well as in specific countries throughout the world.

In considering the licensing of technology, remember that foreign licensees may attempt to use the licensed technology to manufacture products in direct competition with the licenser or its other licensees. In many instances, U.S. licensers may wish to impose territorial restrictions on their foreign licensees, depending on U.S. and foreign antitrust laws as well as the licensing laws of the host country. Also, U.S. and foreign patent, trademark, and copyright laws can often be used to bar unauthorized sales by foreign licensees, provided that the U.S. licenser has valid patent, trademark, or copyright protection in the United States or the other countries.

Many countries, particularly the 27 member states of the European Union, also have strict antitrust laws that affect technology licensing. The European Union has issued a detailed regulation, known as the *block exemption regulation,* governing patent and know-how licensing agreements as well as design and model rights and software copyright licenses. The block exemption regulation is Commission Regulation (EC) No. 772/2004 of April 27, 2004, and deals with the application of article 81(3) of the Treaty of Rome to categories of technology transfer agreements.

If you are currently licensing or contemplating licensing technology to the European Union, you should carefully consider the regulation.

Because of the potential complexity of international technology licensing agreements, your company should seek qualified legal advice in the United States before entering into such an agreement.

In many instances, U.S. licensers should also retain qualified legal counsel in the host country in order to obtain advice on applicable local laws and to receive assistance in securing the foreign government's approval of the agreement. Sound legal advice and thorough investigation of the prospective licensee and the host country will increase the likelihood that your licensing agreement will be a profitable transaction.

JOINT VENTURES

In some cases, joint ventures provide the best partner like manner of obtaining foreign trade income. International joint ventures are used in a wide variety of manufacturing, mining, and service industries, and they frequently involve technology licensing by the U.S. company to the joint venture.

Host country laws may require that a certain percentage (often 51 percent or more) of manufacturing or mining operations be owned by nationals of that country, thereby limiting U.S. companies' local participation to minority shares of joint ventures. Despite such legal requirements, as a U.S. firm you may find it desirable to enter into a joint venture with a foreign firm to help spread the high costs and risks frequently associated with foreign operations. The local partner will likely bring to the joint venture its knowledge of the customs and tastes of local consumers, an established distribution network, and valuable business and political contacts.

There are some possible disadvantages to international joint ventures. A major potential drawback, especially in countries that limit foreign companies to minority participation, is the loss of effective managerial control. As a result, you may experience reduced profits, increased operating costs, inferior product quality, exposure to product liability, and environmental litigation and fines. U.S. firms that wish to retain effective managerial control will find this issue important in negotiations with the prospective joint venture partner and the host government.

Because of the complex legal issues frequently raised by international joint venture agreements, you should seek legal advice from qualified U.S. counsel before entering into such an agreement. Many of the export counseling sources discussed in Chapter 4 can help direct you to legal counsel suitable for your needs.

U.S. companies contemplating international joint ventures should consider retaining experienced counsel in the host country as well. You may be at a disadvantage if you rely on your potential joint venture partners to negotiate host government approvals and to advise you on legal issues, because the interests of the prospective partners may not always coincide with your own. Qualified foreign counsel can be very helpful in obtaining government approvals and providing ongoing advice regarding the host country's intellectual property, tax, labor, corporate, commercial, antitrust, and exchange control laws.

FACT: Companies in a wide variety of industries enter joint ventures as a way of obtaining revenue from overseas operations.

INSIGHT: By forming partnerships or conglomerates, companies can share risk and expertise.

FACT: Domestic and overseas trade shows can help small firms find technology licensing and joint venture opportunities, and U.S. government assistance is also available at many of them.

INSIGHT: German trade shows, both vertical and horizontal, are among the biggest international shows in the world.

Chapter 8: PREPARING YOUR PRODUCT FOR EXPORT

In This Chapter

- **Adapting your product to meet government regulations, country conditions, or preferences**
- **Modifying your product labeling and packaging**
- **Planning for installation of your product overseas**

Selecting and preparing your product for export require not only product knowledge but also knowledge of the unique characteristics of each target market. Market research and contacts with foreign partners, buyers, customers, and others should give your company an idea of what products can be sold and where. However, before the sale can occur, your company may need to modify a particular product to satisfy buyer tastes, needs in foreign markets, or legal requirements for the foreign destination.

The extent to which your company will be willing to modify products sold for export markets is a key policy issue to be addressed by management. Some exporters believe that their domestic products can be exported without significant changes. Others seek to consciously develop uniform products that are acceptable in all markets. It is very important to do research and to be sure of the right strategy to pursue. For example, you may need to redesign an electrical product to run on a different level of voltage for a particular destination, or you may need to redesign packaging to meet labeling standards or cultural preferences.

If your company manufactures more than one product or offers many models of a single product, you should start by exporting the one best suited to the targeted market. Ideally, your company may choose one or two products that fit the target market without major design or engineering modifications. Doing so works best when your company:

- Deals with international customers that have the same demographic characteristics or the same specifications for manufactured goods
- Supplies parts for U.S. goods that are exported to other countries without modifications
- Produces a unique product that is sold on the basis of its status or international appeal
- Produces a product that has few or no distinguishing features and that is sold almost exclusively on a commodity or price basis

QUESTIONS TO CONSIDER

You must consider several issues when you are thinking of selling overseas, including the following:

- What foreign needs does your product satisfy?
- What products should your company offer abroad?
- Should your company modify its domestic-market product for sale abroad? Should it develop a new product for the foreign market?
- What specific features, such as design, color, size, packaging, brand, labels, and warranty, should your product have? How important are languages or cultural differences?
- What specific services are necessary abroad at the presale and post sale stages? Warranties? Spare parts?
- Are your firm's service and repair facilities adequate?

PRODUCT ADAPTATION

To enter a foreign market successfully, your company may have to modify its product to conform to government regulations, geographic and climatic conditions, buyer preferences, or standards of living. Your company may also need to modify its product to facilitate shipment or to compensate for possible differences in engineering and design standards. Foreign government product regulations are common in international trade and are expected to expand in the future. These regulations can take the form of high tariffs, or they can be non-tariff barriers, such as industrial regulations or product specifications. Governments impose these regulations

- To protect domestic industries from foreign competition
- To protect the health and safety of their citizens
- To force importers to comply with environmental controls
- To ensure that importers meet local requirements for electrical or measurement systems
- To restrict the flow of goods originating in or having components from certain countries
- To protect their citizens from cultural influences deemed inappropriate

Detailed information on regulations imposed by foreign countries is available from the Trade Information Center at (800) USA-TRADE (800-872-8723) or from your local Export Assistance Center. When a foreign government imposes particularly onerous or discriminatory barriers, your company may be able to obtain help from the U.S. government to press for their removal. Your firm should contact an Export Assistance Center or the Office of the U.S. Trade Representative (USTR).

Buyer preferences in a foreign market may also lead you to modify your product. Local customs, such as religious practices or the use of leisure time, often determine whether a product is marketable. The sensory impression made by a product, such as taste or visual effect, may also be a critical factor. For example, Japanese consumers tend to prefer certain kinds of packaging, leading many U.S. companies to redesign cartons and packages that are destined for the Japanese market.

Market potential must be large enough to justify the direct and indirect costs involved in product adaptation. Your firm should assess the costs to be incurred and, though it may be difficult, should determine the increased revenues expected from adaptation. The decision to adapt a product is based partly on the degree of commitment to the specific foreign market; a firm with short-term goals will probably have a different perspective than a firm with long-term goals.

ENGINEERING AND REDESIGN

In addition to adaptations related to cultural and consumer preference, your company should be aware that even fundamental aspects of products may require changing. For example, electrical standards in many foreign countries differ from U.S. electrical standards. It's not unusual to find phases, cycles, or voltages (for both residential and commercial use) that would damage or impair the operating efficiency of equipment designed for use in the United States. Electrical standards sometimes vary even within the same country. Knowing the requirements, the manufacturer can determine whether a special motor must be substituted or if a different drive ratio can be achieved to meet the desired operating revolutions per minute.

Similarly, many kinds of equipment must be engineered in the metric system for integration with other pieces of equipment or for compliance with the standards of a given country. The United States is virtually alone in its adherence to a non-metric system, and U.S. firms that compete successfully in the global market realize that conversion to metric measurement is an important detail in selling to overseas customers. Even instruction or maintenance manuals should take care to give dimensions in centimeters, weights in grams or kilos, and temperatures in degrees Celsius. Information on foreign standards and certification systems is available from the National Center for Standards and Certificates Information, National Institute of Standards and Technology, U.S. Department of Commerce, 100 Bureau Dr., M.S. 2150, Gaithersburg, MD 20899-2150.

BRANDING, LABELING, AND PACKAGING

Consumers are concerned with both the product itself and the product's secondary features, such as packaging, warranties, and service. Branding and labeling products in foreign markets raise new considerations for your company, such as the following:

- Are international brand names important to promote and distinguish a product? Conversely, should local brands or private labels be used to heighten local interest?
- Are the colors used on labels and packages offensive or attractive to the foreign buyer? For example, in some countries certain colors are associated with death.
- Can labels and instructions be produced in official or customary languages if required by law or practice?
- Does information on product content and country of origin have to be provided?
- Are weights and measures stated in the local unit? Even with consumer products, packaging and describing contents in metric measurements (e.g., kilograms, liters) can be important.
- Must each item be labeled individually? What is the language of the labeling? For example, "Made in U.S.A." may not be acceptable; the product may need to be labeled in the language spoken by the country's consumers. There may be special labeling requirements for foods, pharmaceuticals, and other products.
- Are local tastes and knowledge considered? A cereal box with the picture of a U.S. athlete on it may not be as attractive to overseas consumers as the picture of a local sports hero.

INSTALLATION

Another element of product preparation that your company should consider is the ease of installing the product overseas. If technicians or engineers are needed overseas to assist in installation, your company should minimize their time in the field if possible. To do so, your company may wish to preassemble or pretest the product before shipping or to provide training for local service providers through the Web, training seminars, or DVDs.

Your company may consider disassembling the product for shipment and reassembling it abroad. This method can save your firm shipping costs, but it may delay payment if the sale is contingent on an assembled product. Your company should be careful to provide all product information, such as training manuals, installation instructions (even relatively simple instructions), and parts lists, in the local language.

WARRANTIES

Your company should consider carefully the terms of a warranty on the product (and be very specific as to the warranty's coverage), because the buyer will expect a specific level of performance and a guarantee that it will be achieved. Levels of expectation and rights for a warranty vary by country, depending on the country's level of development, its competitive practices, the activism of consumer groups, the local standards of production quality, and other factors. Product service guarantees are important because customers overseas typically have service expectations as high or greater than those of U.S. customers.

FACT: Language and cultural factors have played an important role in the success or failure of many exporting efforts.

INSIGHT: Be careful to look into the meanings that your company's (or product's) name may have in other markets. You don't want to discover too late that they are inappropriate in the local language or culture.

FACT: Freight charges are usually assessed by weight or volume.

INSIGHT: Consider shipping items unassembled to reduce delivery costs. Shipping unassembled goods also facilitates movement on narrow roads or through doorways and elevators. Remember, however, that while shipping your items unassembled can save your firm shipping costs, it could delay payment if the sale is contingent on receipt of an assembled product.

Chapter 9: EXPORTING SERVICES

In This Chapter:

- Role of the service sector in the United States and in world economies
- Differences between service and product exporting
- Places where service exporters can find assistance

The United States is the world's premier producer and exporter of services. As the largest component of the U.S. economy, the service sector includes all private-sector economic activity other than agriculture, mining, construction, and manufacturing. The service sector accounts for nearly 80 percent of the private-sector gross domestic product (GDP) and for 90 million jobs.

In the future, the service sector will loom even larger in the U.S. economy. Small and medium-sized entrepreneurial firms—those employing fewer than 500 employees—overwhelmingly lead this service-driven business expansion. There are more than 4 million small service companies that account for more than 16 million jobs. Although small service firms make up most of the service sector, many of the most prominent U.S. service exporters are large firms. Seven of the 30 companies that constitute the widely cited Dow Jones Industrial Average are service firms.

The dominant role that services play throughout the U.S. economy translates into leadership in technology advancement, growth in skilled jobs, and global competitiveness. U.S. service exports more than doubled between 1990 and 2000—increasing from $148 billion in 1990 to $299 billion in 2000. Growth continued to $404 billion in 2006.

In 2004, U.S. service exports exceeded imports by $80 billion, offsetting 10 percent of the deficit in merchandise trade. U.S. services compete successfully worldwide. Major markets for U.S. services include the European Union ($140 billion), Japan ($41 billion), and Canada ($39 billion). At $22 billion, Mexico is the largest emerging market for U.S. service exports.

SERVICE EXPORTS WITH HIGH GROWTH POTENTIAL

The following sectors have grown most rapidly because of technology development and have particularly high export potential:

- **Travel and tourism.** The largest single category within the U.S. service sector encompasses all travel- and tourism-related businesses. As such, recreational and cultural services are included. The industry is diverse and encompasses services in transportation, lodging, food and beverage, recreation, and purchase of incidentals consumed while in transit. Export sales for this sector in 2006 were $86 billion.

- **Environmental services.** The environmental technologies industry is defined generally as all goods and services that generate revenue associated with environmental protection, assessment, compliance with environmental regulations, pollution control, waste management, remediation of contaminated property, design and operation of environmental infrastructure, and provision and delivery of environmental resources. The industry has evolved in response to growing concern about the risks and costs of pollution and to the enactment of pollution control legislation in the United States and around the world. The United States is the largest producer and consumer of environmental technologies in the world.

- **Transportation services.** This sector encompasses aviation, ocean shipping, inland waterways, railroads, trucking, pipelines, and intermodal services, as well as ancillary and support services in ports, airports, rail yards, and truck terminals. Transportation is the indispensable service for international trade in goods, moving all manufactured, mining, and agricultural products to market as well as transporting people engaged in business, travel, and tourism. For 2006, total export sales for transportation services were more than $68 billion.

- **Banking, financial, and insurance services.** U.S. financial institutions are very competitive internationally, particularly when offering account management, credit card operations, and collection management. U.S. insurers offer valuable services, ranging from underwriting and risk evaluation to insurance operations and management contracts in the international marketplace. This sector was a $52 billion export market in 2006.

- **Telecommunications and information services.** This sector includes companies that generate, process, and export electronic commerce activities, such as e-mail, funds transfer, and data interchange, as well as data processing, network services, electronic information services, and professional computer services. The

United States leads the world in marketing new technologies and enjoys a competitive advantage in computer operations, data processing and transmission, online services, computer consulting, and systems integration. Export sales in this sector also totaled more than $16 billion in 2006.

- **Education and training services.** Management training, technical training, and English language training are areas in which U.S. expertise remains unchallenged. The export market for such training is almost limitless, encompassing most industry sectors for products and services. Export sales were almost $15 billion in 2006 for this sector.

- **Commercial, professional, and technical services.** This sector encompasses accounting, advertising, and legal and management consulting services. The international market for those services is expanding at a more rapid rate than the U.S. domestic market. Organizations and business enterprises all over the world look to U.S. firms as leaders in these sectors for advice and assistance. This sector represented $13 billion in export sales in 2006.

- **Entertainment.** U.S.-filmed entertainment and U.S.-recorded music have been very successful in appealing to audiences worldwide. U.S. film companies license and sell rights to exhibit films in movie theaters, on television, on videocassettes, and on DVDs and CDs. U.S. music has been successful in both English-speaking and non-English-speaking countries. The entertainment sector had more than $11 billion in export sales in 2006.

- **Architectural, construction, and engineering services.** The vast experience and technological leadership of the U.S. construction industry, as well as special skills in operations, maintenance, and management, frequently give U.S. firms a competitive edge in international projects. U.S. firms with expertise in specialized fields, such as electric-power utilities, construction, and engineering services, are similarly competitive. Exports for this sector were about $5 billion in 2006.

- E-business. This sector, which can be service or product oriented, is expected to grow dramatically. It is estimated that there are already 400 million Internet users worldwide—but that figure represents only about 7 percent of the world's population.

ASPECTS OF SERVICE EXPORTS

Services can be crucial in stimulating goods exports and are critical in maintaining those transactions. Many U.S. merchandise exports would not take place if they were not supported by service activities such as banking, insurance, and transportation. There are many obvious differences between services and products, including differences in tangibility and customer involvement (see Box 9.1). Because services are intangible, you may find that communicating a service offer is more difficult than communicating a product offer. Also, services frequently must be tailored to the specific needs of the client. Such adaptation often necessitates the client's direct participation and cooperation. Involving the client requires the service provider to possess interpersonal skills and cultural sensitivity.

The intangibility of services makes financing somewhat more difficult—given that no form of collateral is involved—and financial institutions may be less willing to provide financial support to your company. However, many public and private institutions will provide financial assistance to creditworthy service exporters. Trade organizations offer two important finance services under various terms and conditions. One is a guarantee program that requires the participation of an approved lender; the other program provides loans or grants to the exporter or a foreign government. Exporters who insure their accounts receivable against commercial credit and political risk loss are usually able to secure financing from commercial banks and other institutions at lower rates and on a more liberal basis than would otherwise be the case.

MARKETING SERVICES ABROAD

Because service exports may be delivered in support of product exports, you might find it sensible to follow the path of complementary product exports. For years, many large accounting and banking firms have exported by following their major international clients abroad and continuing to assist them in their international activities. Smaller service exporters who cooperate closely with manufacturing firms are operating internationally and aim to provide service support for those manufacturers abroad.

Also, your service firm may seek affiliation with a foreign firm. An agent, representative, or joint venture relationship could prove beneficial to your firm. An indigenous service firm already has knowledge of the various aspects of marketing in a particular country, such as regulations, restrictions, primary participants, potential clients, and competitors. The indigenous firm will also have market research, exposure, and contacts that you can use to your advantage.

OBTAINING GOVERNMENT SUPPORT FOR SERVICE EXPORTS

The Manufacturing and Services unit of the Department of Commerce's International Trade Administration provides support to U.S. services exporters by conducting policy research and industry analysis, coordinating advisory committees, and advocating for U.S. interests in trade negotiations. The U.S. Commercial Service, through the network of domestic U.S. Export Assistance Centers, provides counseling and assistance to services exporters.

FACT: More than two-thirds of U.S. small and medium-sized exporters are non-manufacturers.

INSIGHT: You don't have to be a manufacturer to export.

FACT: In the coming decade, the service sector is forecast to account for almost all net gains in U.S. employment, with small, medium-sized, and large companies all playing key roles in capital formation, business expansion, and new jobs.

INSIGHT: Small firms make up most of the service sector, and small service firms will play a vital role in job growth.

Chapter 10: INTERNATIONAL LEGAL CONSIDERATIONS

In This Chapter

- **Regulations you must follow to comply with U.S. law**
- **Procedures to ensure a successful export transaction**
- **Programs and tax procedures that open new markets and provide you with financial benefits**
- **Intellectual property considerations**

EXPORT REGULATIONS

The Export Administration Regulations (EAR) govern the export and reexport of items for reasons of national security, non-proliferation, foreign policy, and short supply. A relatively small percentage of exports and reexports require the submission of a license application to the U.S. Department of Commerce's Bureau of Industry and Security (BIS). Licensing is dependent on an item's technical characteristics, destination, end use, and end user. Once a classification has been determined, exporters may use a single chart, set forth in the EAR, to decide if a license is needed to export to a particular country. The regulations include answers to frequently asked questions, detailed step-by-step instructions for finding out if a transaction is subject to the regulations, instructions for requesting a commodity classification or advisory opinion, and directions for applying for a license. If you have questions about whether your products require a license, call your local Export Assistance Center or (800) USA-TRADE (800-872-8723).

Antidiversion Clause

To help ensure that U.S. exports go only to legally authorized destinations, the U.S. government requires a destination control statement on shipping documents. The commercial invoice and bill of lading (or air waybill) for nearly all commercial shipments leaving the United States must display a statement notifying the carrier and all foreign parties (the ultimate and intermediate consignees and purchaser) that the U.S. material has been approved for export only to certain destinations and may not be diverted. The minimum antidiversion statement for goods exported under U.S. Department of Commerce authority says, "These commodities, technology, or software were exported from the United States in accordance with the Export Administration Regulations. Diversion contrary to U.S. law is prohibited."

Exceptions to the use of the destination control statement are listed in Part 758.6 of the EAR. Advice on the appropriate statement to use can be provided by the U.S. Department of Commerce, an attorney, or the freight forwarder.

Antiboycott Regulations

The United States has an established policy of opposing restrictive trade practices or boycotts fostered or imposed by foreign countries against other countries friendly to the United States. This policy is implemented through the antiboycott provisions of the Export Administration Act (enforced by the U.S. Department of Commerce) and through a 1977 amendment to the Tax Reform Act of 1976 (enforced by the U.S. Department of the Treasury). In general, these laws prohibit U.S. persons from participating in foreign boycotts or taking actions that further or support such boycotts. The antiboycott regulations carry out this general purpose by:

- Prohibiting U.S. agencies or persons from refusing to do business with blacklisted firms and boycotted friendly countries pursuant to foreign boycott demands
- Prohibiting U.S. persons from discriminating against, or agreeing to discriminate against, other U.S. persons on the basis of race, religion, gender, or national origin in order to comply with a foreign boycott
- Prohibiting U.S. citizens from furnishing information about business relationships with boycotted friendly foreign countries or blacklisted companies in response to boycott requirements
- Providing for public disclosure of requests to comply with foreign boycotts
- Requiring U.S. persons who receive requests to comply with foreign boycotts to report receipt of the requests to the U.S. Department of Commerce and to disclose publicly whether they have complied with such requests

Foreign Corrupt Practices Act

Under the Foreign Corrupt Practices Act (FCPA), it is unlawful for a U.S. person or firm (as well as any officer, director, employee, or agent of a firm or any stockholder acting on behalf of the firm) to offer, pay, or promise to pay (or to authorize any such payment or promise) money or anything of value to any foreign official (or foreign political party or candidate for foreign political office) for the purpose of obtaining or retaining business. It is also unlawful to make a payment to any person while knowing that all or a portion of the payment will be offered, given, or promised—directly or indirectly—to any foreign official (or foreign political party or candidate for foreign political office) for the purposes of assisting the firm in obtaining or retaining business. "Knowing" includes the concepts of "conscious disregard" and "willful blindness." The FCPA also covers foreign persons or firms that commit acts in furtherance of such bribery in the territory of the United States. U.S. persons or firms, or covered foreign persons or firms, should consult an attorney when confronted with FCPA issues.

For further information from the U.S. Department of Justice about the FCPA and the FCPA Opinion Procedure, contact the Deputy Chief, Fraud Section, Criminal Division, U.S. Department of Justice, 10th and Constitution Ave., NW, Bond Building, 4th Floor, Washington, DC 20530, or call (202) 514-1721. Specific questions should be faxed to the Foreign Corrupt Practices Act coordinator, Department of Justice, Criminal Division, Fraud Section at (202) 514-7021.

Although the U.S. Department of Commerce has no enforcement role with respect to the FCPA, it supplies general guidance to U.S. exporters who have questions about the law and about international developments concerning it. For further information, contact the Office of Chief Counsel for International Commerce at (202) 482-0937 or view the Web site.

IMPORT REGULATIONS OF FOREIGN GOVERNMENTS

Import documentation requirements and other regulations imposed by foreign governments vary from country to country. As an exporter, you must be aware of the regulations that apply to your own operations and transactions. For instance, many governments require consular invoices, certificates of inspection, health certification, and various other documents.

NORTH AMERICAN FREE TRADE AGREEMENT

The North American Free Trade Agreement (NAFTA) was negotiated among the United States, Mexico, and Canada and came into effect on January 1, 1994. It provides for the elimination of tariffs on most goods originating in the three countries over a maximum transition period of 15 years. An excellent source of information on all aspects of NAFTA is the U.S. Commercial Service's Trade Information Center at (800) USA-TRADE (800-872-8723).

Tariffs will be eliminated only on goods that originate in one of the four ways defined in article 401 of the NAFTA:

- Goods wholly obtained or produced entirely in the NAFTA region
- Goods meeting a specific Annex 401 origin rule
- Goods produced entirely in the NAFTA region exclusively from originating materials
- Unassembled goods and goods whose content does not meet the Annex 401 rule of origin but contains NAFTA regional value of 60 percent according to the transaction value method or 50 percent according to the net-cost method

Article 502 of the NAFTA requires that importers base their claims of the country of origin on the exporters' written certificate of origin, which may be the U.S.-approved certificate of origin (CF 434), the Canadian certificate of origin (Form B-232), or the Mexican certificate of origin (*Certificado de Origen*). The certificate may cover a single shipment, or it may be used as a blanket declaration for a period of 12 months. In either case, the certificate must be in the importer's possession when the importer is making the claim.

U.S. FOREIGN-TRADE ZONES

As an exporter, your company should also consider the customs privileges of U.S. foreign trade zones (FTZs). These zones are domestic U.S. sites that are considered outside U.S. customs territory and are available for activities that might otherwise be carried on overseas for customs reasons. For export operations, the zones provide accelerated export status for purposes of excise tax rebates. There is no issue of drawback because duties are not collected when the goods are in the FTZ. For import and reexport activities, no customs duties, federal excise taxes, or state or local ad valorem taxes are charged on foreign goods moved into FTZs unless and until the goods or products made from them are moved into U.S. customs territory. Thus, FTZs can be profitable for operations involving foreign dutiable materials and components being assembled or produced here for reexport. Also, no quota restrictions ordinarily apply to export activity.

As of January 2006, there were 268 approved FTZs in communities throughout the United States. Associated with these FTZs are more than 400 subzones. These facilities are available for operations involving storage, repacking, inspection, exhibition, assembly, manufacturing, and other processing. The value of merchandise handled by FTZs exceeds $170 billion.

Information about the zones is available from the zone manager, from local Export Assistance Centers, or from the Executive Secretary, Foreign-Trade Zones Board, International Trade Administration, United States Department of Commerce, 1401 Constitution Ave., NW, Suite 4100W, Washington, DC 20230.

EXPORT PROCESSING ZONES

To encourage and facilitate international trade, countries all over the world have established many types of export processing zones (EPZs), which include free trade zones, special economic zones, bonded warehouses, free ports, and customs zones. EPZs have evolved from initial assembly and simple processing activities to include high-tech and science parks, finance zones, logistics centers, and even tourist resorts. They now include not only general type zones but also single-industry zones and single-commodity zones. Both the number of EPZs and the number of countries hosting them have expanded rapidly. There are now more than 600 EPZs in more than 100 countries. Many U.S. manufacturers and their distributors use these zones for receiving shipments of goods that are reshipped in smaller lots to customers throughout the surrounding areas. For further information, contact your local Export Assistance Center or the Trade Information Center at (800) USA-TRADE (800-872-8723).

CUSTOMS-BONDED WAREHOUSES

A customs-bonded warehouse is a building or other secured area in which dutiable goods may be stored, may be manipulated, or may undergo manufacturing operations without payment of duty. Authority for establishing bonded-storage warehouses is set forth in Title 19, *United States Code* (*U.S.C.*), section 1555. Bonded manufacturing and smelting and refining warehouses are established under Title 19, *U.S.C.*, sections 1311 and 1312.

When goods enter a bonded warehouse, the importer and warehouse proprietor incur financial and legal liability under a bond. The liability is canceled when the goods are:

- Exported
- Withdrawn for supplies to a vessel or aircraft in international traffic
- Destroyed under U.S. Customs supervision
- Withdrawn for consumption within the United States after payment of duty

Your company could enjoy several advantages by using a bonded warehouse. No duty is collected until merchandise is withdrawn for consumption. An importer has control over use of money until the duty is paid on withdrawal of merchandise from the bonded warehouse. If no domestic buyer is found for the imported articles, the importing company can sell merchandise for exportation, thereby canceling the importer's obligation to pay duty.

Many items subject to quota or other restrictions may be stored in a bonded warehouse.

Check with the nearest U.S. Customs office, however, before placing such merchandise in a bonded warehouse.

Duties owed on articles that have been manipulated are determined at the time of withdrawal from the bonded warehouse.

INTELLECTUAL PROPERTY CONSIDERATIONS

Intellectual property refers to a broad collection of rights relating to works of authorship, which are protected under copyright law; inventions, which are protected under patent law; marks, which are protected by trademark law; and designs and trade secrets. No international treaty completely defines these types of intellectual property, and countries' laws differ in significant respects. National intellectual property laws create, confirm, or regulate a property right without which others could use or copy a trade secret, an expression, a design, or a product or its mark and packaging.

The rights granted by a U.S. patent, trademark registration, copyright, or mask work (design of a semiconductor chip) registration extend only throughout the United States and its territories and possessions. They confer no protection on your company's product in a foreign country. There is no such thing as an international patent, trademark, or copyright. To secure patent or mask rights in any country, you must apply for the patent or register the mask work in that country. While most countries require registration of trademarks in order to secure protection, others grant rights that are based on priority of use in that country. Copyright protection depends on national laws, but registration is typically not required. There is no real shortcut to worldwide protection of intellectual property. However, some advantages and minimum standards for the protection and enforcement of intellectual property exist under treaties or other international agreements.

International Agreements

The oldest treaty relating to patents, trademarks, and unfair competition is the Paris Convention for the Protection of Industrial Property. The United States and more than 160 other countries are parties to this treaty. The Paris Convention sets minimum standards of protection and provides two important benefits: the right of national treatment and the right of priority.

In a general sense, *national treatment* means that a Paris Convention country will not discriminate against nationals of another Paris Convention country in granting patent or trademark protection. The rights provided by a foreign country may be greater or less than those provided under U.S. law, but the rights given will be the same as that country provides to its own citizens.

Before the existence of the Paris Convention, it was difficult to obtain protection for industrial property rights in the various countries of the world because of the diversity of their laws. Furthermore, patent applications had to be made roughly at the same time in all countries in order to avoid publication in one country destroying the novelty of the invention in the other countries. In addition, a delay in filing a patent or trademark application left open the possibility that those rights would be lost because of intervening acts such as sale of the invention or registration of the trademark by another person. The Paris Convention's right of priority provides a solution to that problem by establishing an alternative to filing applications in many countries simultaneously. It allows the applicant one year from the date of the first application filed in a Paris Convention country (six months for a design or trademark) in which to file in other countries. Publication or sale of an invention, or use of a mark, after first filing will therefore not jeopardize patentability in countries that grant a right of priority to U.S. applicants as long as they submit an application before the end of the priority period.

Not all countries adhere to the Paris Convention, but similar benefits may be available under another treaty or bilateral agreement. These substantive obligations have been incorporated into the World Trade Organization (WTO) Agreement on Trade-Related Aspects of Intellectual Property Rights (TRIPs) and must be adhered to by WTO members.

The United States is also a party to the Patent Cooperation Treaty (PCT), which provides procedures for filing patent applications in its member countries. The PCT allows you to file one international application that designates member countries in which a patent is sought. Filing the international application extends the period in which you have to fulfill the national requirements for each country by 18 months. This additional time can be very useful for evaluating the chances of obtaining patents and of exploiting your invention commercially in various designated countries. It is also useful for assessing both the technical value of your invention and the continued need for protection in those countries. Only after you have decided whether, and with respect to which countries, you wish to proceed further with your application must you fulfill the various national requirements for entry into the national phase. These requirements include paying national fees and, in some cases, filing translations of the application was filed or as amended.

The international copyright regulations that the United States abides by are governed principally by the Berne Convention for the Protection of Literary and Artistic Works, to which about 160 other nations adhere. The United States is also a member of the Universal Copyright Convention (UCC) and has special bilateral relations with a number of foreign countries. Under the Berne Convention, works created by a national of a Berne Union country or works first or simultaneously published in a Berne country are automatically eligible for protection in every other country of the Berne Union, without registration or compliance with any other formality of law.

These rules hold true of works first published in the United States on or after March 1, 1989, the date on which the United States acceded to the Berne Convention. Works first published before March 1989 were protected in many countries under the UCC – if the works were published with the formalities specified in that convention. Older works may also be protected as a consequence of simultaneous publication in a Berne country or by virtue of bilateral obligations. In any event, the requirements and protection vary from country to country; you should investigate them before seeking publication anywhere.

North American Free Trade Agreement and Agreement on Trade-Related Aspects of Intellectual Property Rights

Both NAFTA and TRIPs establish minimum standards for the protection of intellectual property and the enforcement of those standards. Neither agreement bestows rights on U.S. intellectual property owners. Rather, both agreements ensure that a member state that is party to one or both of the agreements provides a certain level of protection to those individuals or companies protected under that member state's laws.

Patent Law

U.S. patent law differs from the patent laws of most other countries in several important aspects. U.S. patent law grants a patent to the first inventor, even if another person independently makes the invention and files an application first. Most other countries award the patent to the inventor who first files a patent application. The United States also provides a one-year grace period that does not preclude an inventor from obtaining protection after an act such as publishing, offering for sale, or using the invention that would make the invention public. Many countries, including most European countries, lack a grace period that allows an inventor to so disclose an invention before filing a patent application. In countries with an absolute novelty rule, the inventor must file a patent application before making the invention public anywhere. Hence, even the publication of an invention in a U.S. patent grant is a disclosure that can defeat the right to obtain foreign patents unless the applicant is entitled to claim the right of priority under the Paris Convention, as described.

Unlike the United States, many countries require that an invention be worked locally to retain the benefit of the patent. Working a patent may require commercial-scale manufacture within the country, or it may be met by importation of goods covered by the patent, depending on the law of a particular country. The Paris Convention permits penalties for abuses of patent rights, such as not working a patent—for example, the right to a compulsory license at a reasonable royalty followed by possible forfeiture of the patent when the grant of a compulsory license was not sufficient to prevent abuses.

For an invention made in the United States, U.S. law prohibits filing abroad without a foreign filing license from the Patent and Trademark Office unless six months have elapsed since a U.S. application was filed. This prohibition protects against transfers of information that might damage the national security. The penalties for filing abroad without following these requirements range from loss of U.S. patent rights to possible imprisonment if classified information is released. In addition, other export control laws require you to obtain a license before exporting certain technologies, even if no patent application is filed—or they may bar the exporting of certain technologies altogether.

Trademark Law

A *trademark* is a word, symbol, name, slogan, or combination thereof that identifies and distinguishes the source of sponsorship of goods and may serve as an index of quality. *Service marks* perform the same function for businesses dealing in services rather than goods. For example, an airplane manufacturer might register its service mark. In the United States, rights to trademarks, service marks, and other marks (such as collective marks) are acquired through use in commerce within the United States. (A company may register its mark in the United States based on such use.) Additionally, the United States provides for protection of a mark, registered or not, if that mark has become well known through domestic or international use. However, in most countries, trademark rights are acquired only through registration, and many countries require local use of the registered mark to maintain the registration. Whether a given mark can be registered in a particular country will depend on the law of that country. For example, some countries do not protect service marks. The United States is not a member of any agreement under which a single filing will provide international protection, although the right of priority under the Paris Convention confers a substantial benefit.

If your business is expanding, you may face a period of time in which your mark may be known and perhaps registered in the United States, but you are not quite ready to do business abroad. It is prudent to decide early where you will need trademark protection and to protect your rights by filing in those countries. Where to file is a business decision, balancing the expense of registration against its benefit. At a minimum, you will want to file in countries in which you will do business. You may also find it desirable to file in countries that are known sources of counterfeit goods, although some require local use to maintain a registration. Although trademark laws impose no deadlines for registering a mark, a business should, as a practical matter, register promptly to avoid having its mark registered by someone else.

Although you are not legally required to do so, you may find it helpful to investigate the connotation of a trademark, trade name, number, or trade dress before making a major investment in another country. A different language or culture may have unfavorable, silly, or even rude meanings for words or symbols with neutral or favorable connotations in the United States. Even packaging colors may connote different meanings in different countries. For example, white may imply purity in the United States, but it is the color of mourning in most of the Far East.

Trade names are also protected on a country-by-country basis. Although the Paris Convention requires protection of trade names; they are not necessarily registered as they are in the United States. Each country protects trade names in accordance with its own business practices.

Copyright Law

A *copyright* protects original works of authorship. In the United States, this protection gives the owner the exclusive right to reproduce the work, to prepare derivative works, to distribute copies, or to perform or display the work publicly.

In the United States, original works of authorship include literary, dramatic, musical, artistic, and certain other intellectual works. A computer program, for example, is considered a literary work protected by copyright in the United States and in a large and increasing number of foreign countries.

In most countries, the place of first publication determines if copyright protection is available. Some countries require certain formalities to maintain copyright protection. Many other countries, particularly member countries of the Berne Union, offer copyright protection without these formalities. Still others offer little or no protection for the works of foreign nationals. Before publishing a work anywhere, you should investigate the scope of protection available, as well as the specific legal requirements for copyright protection in countries where you desire copyright protection.

FACT: Failure to understand and fully comply with laws and regulations related to restricted or prohibited exports may result in substantial penalties.

INSIGHT: You must be diligent in your efforts to comply. Contact the U.S. Commercial Service's Trade Information Center to learn more about restricted or prohibited exports by calling (800) USA-TRADE (800-872-8723).

FACT: Trademark laws impose no deadline for registering a mark.

INSIGHT: A business should, as a practical matter, register promptly to avoid having its mark registered by someone else.

Chapter 11: GOING ONLINE: E-EXPORTING TOOLS FOR SMALL BUSINESSES

In This Chapter

- **E-commerce defined**
- **Your company's readiness**
- **Steps to going online**

Global Web use is booming, and millions of new buyers are logging on each year. Electronic commerce, especially business-to-consumer (B2C) e-commerce, reflects this growth.

The Internet's global reach is a cost-effective means for marketing products and services overseas. Companies that establish a corporate Web site publicizing their products and services are able to create an electronic mechanism for safe and secure electronic transactions, to track orders, to provide customer service interface, and to list products' technical specifications. Small and medium-sized companies can broaden their market presence internationally by adopting e-commerce or electronic business practices that are user friendly for non-English-speaking users.

What is electronic commerce? It is buying and selling online through the Internet. The transaction is completed through an electronic network featuring computer systems—the vendor's, a Web host's, and the buyer's—all of which are linked to the Internet.

USE OF ELECTRONIC COMMERCE FOR INTERNATIONAL BUSINESS AND TRADE

Using the Internet to transact business in the global marketplace offers significant advantages to the small or medium-sized company seeking new outlets for its products and services. More than 1 billion people throughout the world have access to the Internet. This presence offers a tremendous potential customer base for the entrepreneur. At the same time, business-to-business (B2B) e-commerce has also surged. Corporations in Africa, Asia, Europe, and Latin America are increasingly migrating many of their marketing programs online to seek new business in regions and countries that they had previously thought to be beyond their resources. They also seek new supply sources and services to meet their internal needs and partners to share manufacturing and marketing responsibilities. Some companies, such as GE, have migrated all their sourcing and bidding processes to the Internet.

For certain industries, products, and services, going online reduces variable costs associated with international marketing. Handling tasks such as order processing, payment, after-sales service, marketing (direct e-mail), and advertising online may lower the international market development costs that an enterprise would incur had it used conventional "brick-and-mortar" market penetration strategies. You should be aware of one important caveat: although English is spoken in many countries, it is still important to consider using the languages prevalent in the countries targeted in your company's e-business strategy. Your Web site should be designed to reach the widest audience in the languages of that audience.

In the context of the Internet, electronic commerce needs to be viewed beyond the traditional commercial arena. E-commerce affects marketing, production, and consumption. Information gathered from customers through Internet stores can be used to customize products, to forecast demand, and to prepare business strategies. Consumers not only pay online for products and services but also search for information about products, negotiate with vendors, and reveal their preferences through their purchasing patterns.

E-commerce offers much promise to U.S. firms interested in using the Internet as another vehicle for exporting. However, you should be familiar with the steps necessary to make your firm's Web site e-export capable. Many U.S. companies have a Web site that fulfills one or more marketing functions tailored to their business specialties. These sites feature at least one of the following characteristics:

- **Transactional site.** A transactional site may be an electronic storefront for a brick-and-mortar retailer or a catalog business, or it may be a showroom for a manufacturer wishing to sell directly to the public. Transactional sites conduct full "end-to-end" transactions through the Web site, allowing customers to search for, order, and pay for products online, as well as allowing them to contact the company for after-sales service. The most sophisticated sites create efficiencies by integrating the transaction process with back-office systems such as accounting, inventory, service, and sales.
- **Information delivery site.** This kind of site generates sales by promoting corporate awareness rather than facilitating online transactions. Its function is similar to a brochure that provides information about the product or service and gives contact information on how to proceed with a purchase. Because such a site is often static and doesn't require the software systems necessary for online transactions, it is less expensive to design and maintain than a transactional site. An information delivery site is ideal for companies that market products and services that cannot be provided online or goods that cannot be sold online. A modified version of this kind of site permits the buyer to shop online for the best price from competing vendors providing the identical product—for example, authorized car manufacturers. Information on options available for a particular model allows the buyer to visualize the configuration and obtain an estimated price for the vehicle.

- **E-marketplaces.** These sites are market-makers because they bring buyers and sellers together to facilitate transactions. Participation in a brokerage often provides an efficient way of finding a customer without the expense of building a proprietary transactional Web site. Types of brokerages include auctions, virtual malls, and matching services.

MARKET DEVELOPMENT ON THE WEB

As with brick-and-mortar enterprises, market development is an essential ingredient for all types of Web sites and must be an integral part of your firm's e-business presence on the Internet. Your company should consider and evaluate the advantages of advertising online as an extension and a component of your corporate growth strategies. Advertising messages often appear on portals or on other Web sites that draw viewers with content (e.g., news and information) and services (e.g., e-mail, chat, and forums). You may seek to advertise on search engines that attract high traffic volume or to target a specialized demographic. Some portals sell favorable link positioning or advertising keyed to particular search terms in a user query. Companies may also consider using an advertising network that feeds ads to a network of sites, thereby enabling large marketing campaigns. These options are available in the United States and internationally in English or in other languages.

Direct e-mail is an inexpensive and efficient way to reach thousands of potential customers. Direct e-mail can be used to promote and enhance Web presence, depending on the market, product, or service. However, several countries have legislation affecting unsolicited commercial e-mail that direct marketers must be aware of. The Direct Marketing Association suggests that direct e-mail messages should have (a) an honest subject line; (b) no forged headers or technological deceptions; (c) the identity of the sender, which includes a physical address; and (d) a visible opt-out clause that is easy to use. Before using direct e-mail to promote Web presence, your company should be aware of the potential for backlash against unsolicited e-mails by consumers who feel overwhelmed by the number of such e-mails they receive. Companies should consult the Controlling the Assault of Non-Solicited Pornography and Marketing (CAN-SPAM) Act of 2003 to ensure full compliance with the law.

TOOLS TO ASSESS YOUR FIRM'S READINESS TO GO ONLINE

Companies that have decided to have a Web presence must assess whether they have the most efficient information technology (IT) solutions to execute their online exporting programs and objectives. IT embodies a range of computer systems and software applications for managing a firm's Web site. With more and more cyber attacks on government and corporate sites, your company should consider investing in security technologies to protect you and your customers from identify theft and denial of service.

An IT assessment should answer the following questions:

- What is your firm's current IT usage? Is it at capacity, and what are the plans for additional IT investment to upgrade existing systems?
- What business applications are best suited to move online for B2B or B2C e-commerce?
- Have you done a cost-benefit analysis of all possible projects involving IT?
- Have you identified current and future security issues, and do you have an action plan for correcting problems?

The U.S. Department of Commerce, through the National Institute of Standards and Technology, has created a tool to assist companies with IT assessment. Called the eScan Security Assessment, the tool is available free of charge. It assesses the electronic security infrastructure of a small or medium-sized business and provides an action plan for improvement. It asks specific questions regarding the following:

- Virus protection
- Physical environment
- Mechanical failure
- Information technology and security policies
- Internet and e-commerce transactions
- File permissions
- Back-up policies and contingency planning
- International concerns
- Operating systems

Once the questions have been answered, the eScan Security Assessment tool produces a detailed report on how well an organization scores in all of those critical security areas. The tool recommends specific steps to correct uncovered security holes, thus enabling companies to build a more secure business model for future Internet strategies.

STEPS TO GOING ONLINE

Potential customers must know who you are and how to reach you. Then, if they want to buy what your company has to sell, you have to facilitate the exchange of money for your product.

Selecting a Domain Name

A key component to establishing a Web presence is choosing a uniform resource locator (URL) and a domain name. As with URLs aimed toward the domestic market, a URL for an online exporter's Web site should be short, simple, descriptive, and memorable to customers in the target market. URL registration is concurrent with domain name registration. Every country (plus a few territories) has a reserved, two-letter country-code domain (e.g., the United Kingdom has the domain ".uk"). An online exporter may choose domain names localized for the target markets. Locally branded domain names may increase brand awareness and Web site address recall, and they may even influence brand sales and loyalty. In addition, most local search engines display only locally relevant content by filtering the search results to include only local country-code domains. If your company wants to have a local domain name, you must research the rules for the particular country, as registration requirements vary.

If your company is seeking foreign customers, you may also consider an internationalized or multilingual domain name. Such domain names are Web addresses written in characters other than the Roman alphabet. For example, a company called Bright Light Bulbs that wishes to sell in China could have a domain name that would use the Chinese characters for Bright Light Bulbs in its Web site address. Internationalized or multilingual domain names allow customers to search and access sites in their native language.

Registering at Search Engines

Most people use search engines to find information on the Internet, so Web site registration with multiple search engines is key to visibility. Search engines range from those that are global in scope to search tools that are focused on small areas of information. Online exporters should register with search engines that are popular with the target audience in their target markets.

Choosing a Web Host

A Web host is a company with a server that maintains the files of Web sites. A variety of free and subscription-based Web-hosting services are available, including those offered by many Internet service providers. Web-hosting services often go beyond Web site maintenance to include domain name registration, Web site design, and search engine registration. For some online exporters, it may be most feasible to use a Web host in their target market to take advantage of all the localized services the host offers. The location or nationality of the Web site host does not affect accessibility of the site; however, when choosing a host, your company should ensure that the host's servers reside within a stable infrastructure and are maintained for optimal reliability.

Localizing and Internationalizing Web Site Content

Companies seeking foreign audiences with their Web sites will want to either localize or internationalize their sites. They may also provide a mixture of both processes. Localization consists of adapting one's Web site to meet the linguistic, cultural, and commercial requirements of a targeted market. Internationalizing a Web site enables a company to be multilingual and sensitive to cultural conventions without the need for extensive redesign. Localization or internationalization must be part of the online exporter's corporate strategy for Web site and business development. Among the features that your company should consider are the following:

- Language
- Cultural nuances, such as differences in color association and symbols
- Payment preferences
- Pricing in the appropriate currency
- Currency converter
- Metric measurements

You can find more information on localization and internationalization at the Web site for the Localization Industry Standards Association.

Promoting Your Site

Setting up shop is no guarantee that customers will come flooding in. If you want a successful site, you can't wait for people to stumble across it. There are a number of ways to promote your site without spending a lot of money:

- Consider purchasing an ad for a nominal cost on BuyUSA.gov, a network of Web sites operated by the U.S. Commercial Service and targeted at foreign buyers.
- Depending on the business you are in, send brief stories about your company and Web site to trade publications that serve the larger industry or business sector in the country market you are targeting.
- Put your domain name on business cards, letterheads, envelopes, packaging, and promotional materials of all kinds.
- Ask foreign visitors if they'd like to receive occasional "opt- in" ads, which are essentially e-mails promoting upcoming sales or new products. Encourage those visitors who consent to receiving the opt-in ads to e-mail them to a friend or relative. People who agree to receive opt-in ads tend to purchase up to seven times as frequently as other visitors.

- Consider sending people who visited or registered on your Web site but didn't buy anything a follow-up e-mail with a coupon for a discount on your products and services.

EXECUTING ORDERS AND PROVIDING AFTER-SALES SERVICE

Guidelines for order execution and after-sales service are similar for offline and online transactions. Therefore, companies planning to export through the Internet should be knowledgeable about the topics discussed in previous chapters. Companies engaging in e-commerce should also consider the following pertinent issues:

Payment Modes and Terms

Companies that use the Internet to reach overseas customers frequently use their Web site to process orders and accept payments. Payment practices vary from country to country. It is important that you identify and incorporate the prevalent payment mechanisms into the order-processing component of the Web site:

- **Credit cards.** For B2C transactions, many overseas customers use credit cards for online purchases, but credit cards are not a universally common method of online payment. To offer credit card payment services, a company must establish a credit card merchant account with a bank. The bank will process the transactions in exchange for a fee. Companies should compare the fee structures of banks to determine which works best for the size and number of transactions expected. The transactions may be fast, but credit cards carry their own risks. Chargebacks can be very costly for online exporters. Common chargeback reasons are fraud, dispute over the quality of merchandise, non-receipt of merchandise, or incorrect amount charged to the card. If your company accepts online credit card transactions, you should be knowledgeable about the credit card issuer's and your bank's policies toward chargebacks and how to avoid them.
- **Account-to-account transfers.** Account-to-account (A2A) transfers, in which money is transferred electronically between the customer's and merchant's banks, are popular in many countries. A2A transactions offer the advantages of occurring in real time and of reducing the potential for fraud and chargebacks. Unfortunately, because A2A transactions are rare in the United States, few U.S. banks offer this service.
- **Person-to-person transfers.** Many companies offer person-to-person (P2P) transfers, in which funds are sent electronically to a third party, which in turn deposits the funds in the merchant's account. An example of a P2P service provider that conducts cross-border transactions is PayPal. PayPal lets anyone with an e-mail address securely send and receive online payments using his or her credit card or bank account. PayPal will

also conduct currency exchange, allowing the customer and merchant to operate in their preferred currency. Google Checkout offers similar service. Other P2P providers, such as Western Union's BidPay, accept a credit card payment from the payer and send a money order to the payee.

Shipping and Pricing

The process of shipping and pricing goods purchased over the Internet is identical to the process for goods purchased by other means, except for digital products (e.g., music, videos, games, or software) that are downloaded from a Web site.

Customer Service

As with offline exporters, online exporters must have an effective customer service program to build and maintain a customer base. Online business poses unique challenges and opportunities for customer service. Customer service should be integral to Web site design and overall business strategy. Online exporters should consider providing the following information and services:

- A list of frequently asked questions (FAQs)
- An online interface for customers to track orders
- Clearly posted contact information (e.g., address, phone number, and e-mail)
- Delivery of timely (e.g., four hours), personalized response s to customer inquiries
- Customer testimonials
- Contact information fields to collect foreign address contact information
- Toll free phone numbers that include Canada
- Information presented in languages other than English

Taxation

Taxation is as relevant to online merchants as to brick-and-mortar businesses. In general, for most overseas markets, a company must have a permanent establishment in a foreign country before that country can subject the company to its general tax jurisdiction. Thus, an American online vendor of digitally or physically delivered goods that does not have equipment or personnel in Japan would not be subject to Japanese taxation. However, there are important exceptions to this general rule. On July 1, 2003, the European Union (EU) member states began taxing sales of electronically supplied goods and services from non-EU firms to customers located in the European Union. Non-EU providers of electronic goods and services are now required to register with a tax authority in the member state of their choosing and to collect and remit value added tax (VAT) at the VAT rate of the member state where their customer is located. Although the EU countries have been the first to move toward a system of taxing electronic sales according to customer location (regardless of where the vendor is established), other countries may soon follow suit. Therefore, if your company exports online, you must know about the tax requirements of your target market.

OTHER IMPORTANT SALES CONSIDERATIONS

For an international Web site, there are a number of additional factors to consider, particularly as they relate to foreign legal and regulatory requirements.

Privacy

U.S. organizations that collect personally identifiable information online should display their privacy policies prominently and offer choices to their data subjects (e.g., customers, employees, and other business contacts) about how their personal information is used. Customers should have the opportunity to refuse having their personal information shared with others or used for promotional purposes. Many countries have privacy laws, and organizations should take care to comply or they may face prosecution. For example, the European Union prohibits the transfer of personal data to non-EU nations that do not meet the EU "adequacy" standard for privacy protection. The U.S. Department of Commerce, in consultation with the European Commission and the private sector, has developed a safe-harbor framework that provides U.S. organizations with a streamlined means to comply with the EU requirements. Companies may self-certify to the safe harbor through the safe-harbor Web site.

Security

Consumers often cite security concerns for not placing orders over the Internet. Compared with other forms of consumer purchasing, the Internet is safe as long as the online merchant takes prudent business precautions. If your company operates a transactional Web site as part of its exporting business, you should post a security statement to reassure customers.

Electronic Signatures

In legal terms, an online sale is an enforceable contract, a valid and binding agreement. However, in some overseas markets, a contract is only enforceable if it is signed "in writing." Such jurisdictions do not recognize electronic signatures and, in the event of a dispute, would not enforce an agreement made by e-mail or through a Web site. Although many countries have modified their laws to recognize electronic signatures, online exporters should check to be sure their target markets accept electronic signatures. If they do, the next step is to determine which signatures are restricted and which technologies are legally valid.

Unsolicited Commercial E-Mail

Unsolicited commercial e-mail (UCE), also known as *unsolicited bulk e-mails* (UBE) or *spam*, is relevant to international e-commerce because its use is controversial. Many businesses see UCE as a quick and cheap way to promote goods and services to a broad range of potential customers. However, UCE costs individuals and businesses significant amounts of time, money, equipment, and productivity. Many domestic and international jurisdictions have laws about UCE, and violation may result in penalties. (See Box 11.1 for information about U.S. law.) In addition, many e-mail service providers, such as America Online and Yahoo!, have rules of conduct that forbid using their service to send UCE. Visit the Direct Marketing Association Web for more guidance on UCE.

Advertising Content

Most countries have laws about advertising content, which may be applied to Web sites, banner ads, and marketing e-mails sent from the United States. Online exporters should research the advertising laws of their target market before initiating a marketing campaign. If you are an exporter of heavily regulated products and services, such as pharmaceuticals or insurance, you may anticipate disclosure requirements and limitations on claims. Companies should avoid the following:

- Comparative advertising (that is, comparing your company's goods or services with those of a competitor)
- Advertising aimed at children
- Use of images or sounds that may be considered intellectual property and may require the permission of the artist
- Use of lotteries, competitions, contests, games, and betting as part of a promotional offer

The International Chamber of Commerce has guidelines on advertising and marketing on the Internet.

Jurisdiction

Online exporters must be aware that they are doing business in a foreign jurisdiction, which means the laws and regulations of the target market apply to the goods and services being sold. For example, an online exporter of medical equipment should ensure that the equipment has been approved for use in the foreign market. Companies should also be aware that the transaction itself may be under the jurisdiction of the foreign market. In other words, the foreign market's laws regarding contracts may apply.

Good Faith

Dealing in good faith is perhaps more important for online businesses than for brick-and-mortar operations because customers rely heavily on reputation. Moreover, it is illegal in most countries to behave otherwise. If you engage in online business, your company must do the following:

- Use fair business, advertising, and marketing practices.
- Provide accurate, clear, and easily accessible information about the company and its goods and services.
- Disclose full information about the terms, conditions, and costs of the transaction.
- Ensure that consumers know they are making a commitment before closing the deal.
- Address consumer complaints and difficulties quickly and fairly.

For more guidance on online good faith commerce, see the Federal Trade Commission's guide for business.

FACT: The worldwide Internet population equals 1 billion users and continues to grow at about 8 percent per year.

INSIGHT: The Internet allows you to broaden your customer base internationally while reducing many of the costs associated with international marketing.

FACT: Business-to-business e-commerce in China is expecte to increase 81 percent by 2008. India's predicted growth is even higher at 88 percent.

INSIGHT: As e-commerce grows throughout the world, your company will want to be ready to reap the benefits.

FACT: Web sites that take an international audience into account make more international sales.

INSIGHT: Consider these points:

- Include a currency converter
- Use the language of your target audience
- Make navigation simple and visual

Chapter 12: SHIPPING YOUR PRODUCT

In This Chapter

- How international freight forwarders can help you
- How your product should be packed and labeled
- What documentation and insurance you may need
- International shipping companies and what services they offer

The hurdles you have to clear don't end with the sale and the Web site. You still have to get the goods to the buyer, who is often located thousands of miles away where different rules may apply. When shipping a product overseas, you must be aware of packing, labeling, documentation, and insurance requirements and regulations. Make sure that the merchandise is:

- Packed correctly so that it arrives in good condition
- Labeled correctly to ensure that the goods are handled properly and arrive on time at the right place
- Documented correctly to meet U.S. and foreign government requirements, as well as proper collection standards
- Insured against damage, loss, pilferage, and delay

Because of the multitude of considerations involved in physically exporting goods, exporters often receive assistance from their air carrier or freight forwarder to perform those services.

FREIGHT FORWARDERS

An international freight forwarder is an agent for moving cargo to an overseas destination. These agents are familiar with the import rules and regulations of foreign countries, the export regulations of the U.S. government, the methods of shipping, and the documents related to foreign trade. Freight forwarders are licensed by the International Air Transport Association (IATA) to handle air freight and the Federal Maritime Commission to handle ocean freight.

Freight forwarders assist exporters in preparing price quotations by advising on freight costs, port charges, consular fees, costs of special documentation, insurance costs, and the freight forwarders' own handling fees. They recommend the packing methods that will protect the merchandise during transit, or they can arrange to have the merchandise packed at the port or put in containers. If the exporter prefers, freight forwarders can reserve the necessary space on a vessel, aircraft, train, or truck. The cost for their services is a factor that should be included in the price charged to the customer.

Once the order is ready for shipment, freight forwarders should review all documents to ensure that everything is in order. This review is of particular importance with letter-of-credit payment terms. Freight forwarders may also prepare the bill of lading and any special required documentation. After shipment, they can route the documents to the seller, the buyer, or a paying bank. Freight forwarders can also make arrangements with customs brokers overseas to ensure that the goods comply with customs import documentation regulations. A *customs broker* is an individual or company that is licensed to transact customs business on behalf of others. Customs business is limited to those activities involving transactions related to the entry and admissibility of merchandise; its classification and valuation; the payment of duties, taxes, or other charges assessed or collected; and the refund, rebate, or drawback of those charges.

PACKING

Your company should be aware of the demands that international shipping puts on packaged goods. You should also keep four potential problems in mind when designing an export shipping crate: breakage, moisture, pilferage, and excess weight.

Buyers are often familiar with the port systems overseas, so they will sometimes specify packaging requirements. If the buyer does not provide such specifications, be sure the goods are prepared using these guidelines:

- Pack in strong containers that are adequately sealed and filled when possible.
- Make sure the weight is evenly distributed to provide proper bracing in the container, regardless of size.
- Put goods on pallets and, when possible, place them in containers.
- Make packages and packing filler out of moisture-resistant material.
- To avoid pilferage, avoid writing contents or brand names on packages.
- Use straps, seals, and shrink-wrap to safeguard goods.
- Observe any product-specific hazardous materials packing requirements.
- Verify compliance with wood-packaging documentation and markings for fumigation and chemical treatment.

One popular method of shipment is to use containers obtained from carriers or private leasing companies. These containers vary in size, material, and construction. They accommodate most cargo but are best suited for standard package sizes and shapes. Also, refrigerated and liquid-bulk containers are usually readily available. Some containers are no more than semitrailers lifted off their wheels, placed on a vessel at the port of export, and then transferred to another set of wheels at the port of import.

Normally, air shipments require less heavy packing than ocean shipments, though they should still be adequately protected, especially if they are likely to attract pilferage. In many instances, standard domestic packing is acceptable if the product is durable and there is no concern for display packaging. In other instances, high-test (at least 250 pounds per square inch) cardboard or tri-wall construction boxes are preferable.

Finally, transportation costs are determined by volume and weight. Specially reinforced and lightweight packing materials have been developed for exporting to minimize volume and weight while reinforcing the packaging. The proper materials may save money as well as ensure that the goods are properly packed. You should hire a professional firm to pack the products if you are not equipped to do so. This service is usually provided at a moderate cost.

LABELING

Specific marking and labeling are used on export shipping cartons and containers. This labeling:

- Meets shipping regulations
- Ensures proper handling
- Conceals the identity of the contents
- Helps receivers identify shipments
- Ensures compliance with environmental and safety standards

The overseas buyer usually specifies which export marks should appear on the cargo for easy identification by receivers. Products may require many markings for shipment. For example, exporters need to put the following markings on cartons to be shipped:

- Shipper's mark
- Country of origin (in your case, "U.S.A.")
- Weight marking (in pounds and kilograms)
- Number of packages and size of cases (in inches and centimeters)
- Handling marks (i.e., international pictorial symbols) **A BASIC GUIDE TO EXPORTING**
- Cautionary markings, such as "This Side Up" or "Use No Hooks" (in English and in the language of the destination country)
- Port of entry

- Labels for hazardous materials (i.e., universal symbols adopted by the International Air Transport Association and the International Maritime Organization)
- Ingredients (if applicable, also included in the language of the destination country)

DOCUMENTATION

Your company should seriously consider having the freight forwarder handle the documentation that exporting requires. Forwarders are specialists in this process. The following documents are commonly used in exporting, but which of them are necessary in a particular transaction depends on the requirements of the U.S. government and the government of the importing country:

- Air freight shipments are covered by *air waybills,* which can never be made in negotiable form.
- A *bill of lading* is a contract between the owner of the goods and the carrier (as with domestic shipments). For shipment by vessel, there are two types: a straight bill of lading, which is not negotiable and does not give title to the goods, and a negotiable, or shipper's order, bill of lading. The latter can be bought, sold, or traded while the goods are in transit. The customer usually needs an original bill of lading as proof of ownership to take possession of the goods.
- A *commercial invoice* is a bill for the goods from the seller to the buyer. Many governments use commercial invoices to determine the true value of goods when assessing customs duties. Governments that use the commercial invoice to control imports will often specify the invoice's form, content, and number of copies, language to be used, and other characteristics.
- A *consular invoice,* a required document in some countries, describes the shipment of goods and shows information such as the consignor, consignee, and value of the shipment. Certified by the consular official of the foreign country, it is used by the country's customs officials to verify the value, quantity, and nature of the shipment.
- A *certificate of origin,* also a required document in certain nations, is a signed statement as to the origin of the export item. Certificates of origin are usually validated by a semiofficial organization, such as a local chamber of commerce. A certificate may be required even if the commercial invoice contains the same information.
- A *NAFTA certificate of origin* is required for products traded among the signatory countries of the North American Free Trade Agreement (Canada, Mexico, and the United States) if the goods are NAFTA qualified and the importer is claiming zero-duty preference under NAFTA.

- An *inspection certification* is required by some purchasers and countries to attest to the specifications of the goods shipped. The inspection is usually performed by a third party, often an independent testing organization.
- A *dock receipt* and a *warehouse receipt* are used to transfer accountability when the domestic carrier moves the export item to the port of embarkation and leaves it with the shipping line for export.
- A *destination control statement* appears on the commercial invoice and on the air waybill or bill of lading to notify the carrier and all foreign parties that the item can be exported only to certain destinations.
- A *shipper's export declaration* (SED) is used to control exports and is a source document for official U.S. export statistics. SEDs, or their electronic equivalent, are required for shipments when the value of the commodities, classified under any single Schedule B number, exceeds $2,500. SEDs must be prepared and submitted for all shipments, regardless of value, that require an export license or are destined for countries restricted by the Export Administration Regulations. SEDs are prepared by the exporter or the exporter's agent and are delivered to the exporting carrier (e.g., the post office, airline, or vessel line). The exporting carrier will present the required number of copies to the U.S. Customs Service at the port of export. Sample Form 12.6 is an example of the reformatted SED, whose use became mandatory on July 18, 2003. The U.S. Census Bureau's Foreign Trade Division is the controlling agency for this document. The bureau made electronic filing of the SED mandatory on September 1, 2008, using AESDirect. AESDirect is a Web-based application that is available to exporters free of charge. It permits the SED to be filed electronically. You can obtain more information on registering as an AESDirect filer and all filing options at *www.aesdirect.gov*. Often, the SED is prepared as a by-product of another document, the shipper's letter of instructions.
- An *export license* is a government document that authorizes the export of specific goods in specific quantities to a particular destination. This document may be required for most or all exports to some countries. For other countries, it may be required only under special circumstances.
- An *export packing list* is considerably more detailed and informative than a standard domestic packing list. It itemizes the material in each package and indicates the type of package, such as a box, crate, drum, or carton. It also shows the individual net, tare, and gross weights and measurements for each package (in both U.S. and metric systems). Package markings should be shown along with references to identify the shipment. The shipper or forwarding agent uses the list to determine the total shipment weight and volume and whether the correct cargo is being shipped. In addition, U.S. and foreign customs officials may use the list to check the cargo.

- An *insurance certificate* is used to assure the consignee that insurance will cover the loss of or damage to the cargo during transit.

Documentation must be precise because slight discrepancies or omissions may prevent merchandise from being exported, may result in non-payment, or may even result in the seizure of the exporter's goods by U.S. or foreign customs officials. Collection documents are subject to precise time limits and may not be honored by a bank if the time has expired. Most documentation is routine for freight forwarders and customs brokers, but as the exporter, you are ultimately responsible for the accuracy of the necessary documents.

The number and kinds of documents that the exporter must deal with vary according to the destination of the shipment. Because each country has different import regulations, the exporter must be careful to provide all proper documentation.

SHIPPING

The handling of transportation is similar for domestic and export orders. Export marks are added to the standard information on a domestic bill of lading. These marks show the name of the exporting carrier and the latest allowed arrival date at the port of export. Instructions for the inland carrier to notify the international freight forwarder by telephone on arrival should also be included. You may find it useful to consult with a freight forwarder to determine the method of international shipping. Because carriers are often used for large and bulky shipments, you can reserve space on the carrier well before actual shipment date. This reservation is called the *booking contract*.

International shipments are increasingly made on a bill of lading under a multimodal contract. The multimodal transit operator (frequently one of the transporters) takes charge of and responsibility for the entire movement from factory to final destination.

The cost of the shipment, delivery schedule, and accessibility to the shipped product by the foreign buyer are all factors to consider when determining the method of international shipping. Although air carriers may be more expensive, their cost may be offset by lower domestic shipping costs (e.g., using a local airport instead of a coastal seaport) and quicker delivery times. These factors may give the U.S. exporter an edge over other competitors.

Before shipping, your firm should check with the foreign buyer about the destination of the goods. Buyers may want the goods to be shipped to a free trade zone or a free port, where they are exempt from import duties (see Chapter 10).

INSURANCE

Damaging weather conditions, rough handling by carriers, and other common hazards to cargo make insurance an important protection for U.S. exporters. If the terms of sale make you responsible for insurance, your company should either obtain its own policy or insure the cargo under a freight forwarder's policy for a fee. If the terms of sale make the foreign buyer responsible, you should not assume (or even take the buyer's word) that adequate insurance has been obtained. If the buyer neglects to obtain adequate coverage, damage to the cargo may cause a major financial loss to your company.

Shipments by sea are covered by marine cargo insurance. Air shipments may also be covered by marine cargo insurance, or insurance may be purchased from the air carrier. Export shipments are usually covered by cargo insurance against loss, damage, and delay in transit. International agreements often limit carrier liability. Additionally, the coverage is substantially different from domestic coverage. Arrangements for insurance may be made by either the buyer or the seller in accordance with the terms of sale. Exporters are advised to consult with international insurance carriers or freight forwarders for more information. Although sellers and buyers can agree to different components, coverage is usually placed at 110 percent of the CIF (cost, insurance, freight) or CIP (carriage and insurance paid to) value.

TARIFFS

Because tariffs, port handling fees, and taxes can be high, it is very important for you to consider their effects on your product's final cost. Typically, the importer pays the tariffs. Nevertheless, these costs will influence how much the buyer is willing to pay for your product.

MAJOR SHIPPERS

International shipping companies have become an excellent resource for exporters. In addition to transporting bulk freight, they now offer assistance with shipping documentation, warehousing in the foreign market, and—in some cases—payment collection from the foreign buyer.

Chapter 13: PRICING, QUOTATIONS, AND TERMS

In This Chapter

- Determining the best price for your product internationally
- Handling requests for quotations and the pro forma invoice
- Defining the terms of sale

Pricing your product properly, giving complete and accurate quotations, choosing the terms of the sale, and selecting the payment method are four critical elements in selling a product or service overseas. Of the four, pricing can be the most challenging, even for an experienced exporter.

PRICING CONSIDERATIONS

These considerations will help you determine the best price for your product overseas:

- At what price should your firm sell its product in the foreign market?
- What type of market positioning (that is, customer perception) does your company want to convey from its pricing structure?
- Does the export price reflect your product's quality?
- Is the price competitive?
- What type of discount (for example, trade, cash, quantity) and allowances (for example, advertising, trade-offs) should your firm offer its foreign customers?
- Should prices differ by market segment?
- What should your firm do about product-line pricing?
- What pricing options are available if your firm's costs increase or decrease? Is the demand in the foreign market elastic or inelastic?
- Is the foreign government going to view your prices as reasonable or exploitative?
- Do the foreign country's antidumping laws pose a problem?

As in the domestic market, the price at which a product or service is sold directly determines your firm's revenues. It is essential that your company's market research include an evaluation of all the variables that may affect the price range for your product or service. If your firm's price is too high, the product or service will not sell. If the price is too low, export activities may not be sufficiently profitable or may actually create a net loss.

The traditional components for determining proper pricing are costs, market demand, and competition. Each component must be compared with your company's objective in entering the foreign market. An analysis of each component from an export perspective may result in export prices that are different from domestic prices.

It is also very important that you take into account additional costs that are typically borne by the importer. They include tariffs, customs fees, currency fluctuation, transaction costs, and value added taxes (VATs). These costs can add substantially to the final price paid by the importer, sometimes resulting in a total that is more than double the U.S. domestic price.

Foreign Market Objectives

An important aspect of your company's pricing analysis is the determination of market objectives. For example, you may ask whether your company is attempting to penetrate a new market, seeking long-term market growth, or looking for an outlet for surplus production or outmoded products.

Marketing and pricing objectives may be generalized or tailored to particular foreign markets. For example, marketing objectives for sales to a developing nation, where per capita income may be one-tenth of that in the United States, are necessarily different than marketing objectives for sales to Europe or Japan.

Costs

The computation of the actual cost of producing a product and bringing it to market is the core element in determining if exporting is financially viable. Many new exporters calculate their export price by the cost-plus method. In that calculation, the exporter starts with the domestic manufacturing cost and adds administration, research and development, overhead, freight forwarding, distributor margins, customs charges, and profit.

The effect of this pricing approach may be that the export price escalates into an uncompetitive range. Table 13.1 provides a sample calculation. It clearly shows that if an export product has the same ex-factory price as the domestic product has, its final consumer price is considerably higher once exporting costs are included.

Marginal cost pricing is a more competitive method of pricing a product for market entry. This method considers the direct out-of-pocket expenses of producing and selling products for export as a floor beneath which prices cannot be set without incurring a loss. For example, additional costs may occur because of product modification for the export market to accommodate different sizes, electrical systems, or labels. Costs may decrease, however, if the export products are stripped-down versions or made without increasing the fixed costs of domestic production. Thus, many costs that apply only to domestic production, such as domestic labeling, packaging, and advertising costs, are subtracted, as are costs such as research and development expenses if they would have been spent anyway for domestic production.

Other costs should be assessed for domestic and export products according to how much benefit each product receives from such expenditures. Additional costs often associated with export sales include the following:

- Fees for market research and credit checks
- Business travel expenses
- International postage and telephone rates
- Translation costs
- Commissions, training charges, and other costs involving foreign representatives
- Consultant and freight forwarder fees
- Product modification and special packaging costs

After the actual cost of the export product has been calculated, you should formulate an approximate consumer price for the foreign market.

Market Demand

For most consumer goods, per capita income is a good gauge of a market's ability to pay. Some products create such a strong demand (for example, Levi's denim jeans) that even low per capita income will not affect their selling price. Simplifying the product to reduce its selling price may be an answer for your company in markets with low per capita income. Your firm must also keep in mind that currency fluctuations may alter the affordability of its goods. Thus, pricing should try to accommodate wild changes in U.S. and foreign currencies. A relatively weak dollar makes the price of U.S. goods more competitive in many markets around the world, thereby enabling you to compete with domestic producers as well as with other foreign competitors whose production costs are suddenly reflected in their inflated domestic currencies. Your firm should also anticipate the kind of customers who will buy your product. If your firm's primary customers in a developing country are expatriates or are local people with high incomes, a higher price might be feasible even if the average per capita income is low.

Competition

In the domestic market, few companies are free to set prices without carefully evaluating their competitors' pricing policies. This situation is true in exporting and is further complicated by the need to evaluate the competition's prices in each potential export market.

If there are many competitors within the foreign market, you may have little choice but to match the market price or even underprice the product or service in order to establish a market share. If the product or service is new to a particular foreign market, however, it may actually be possible to set a higher price than in the domestic market.

Pricing Summary

In summary, here are the key points to remember when determining your product's price:

- Determine the objective in the foreign market.
- Compute the actual cost of the export product.
- Compute the final consumer price.
- Evaluate market demand and competition.
- Consider modifying the product to reduce the export price.
- Include "non-market" costs, such as tariffs and customs fees.
- Exclude cost elements that provide no benefit to the export function, such as domestic advertising.

QUOTATIONS AND PRO FORMA INVOICES

Many export transactions, particularly initial export transactions, begin with the receipt of an inquiry from abroad that is followed by a request for a quotation. A pro forma invoice is a quotation prepared in the format of an invoice; it is the preferred method in the exporting business.

A quotation describes the product, states a price for it, sets the time of shipment, and specifies the terms of sale and terms of payment. Because the foreign buyer may not be familiar with the product, the description of the product in an overseas quotation usually must be more detailed than in a domestic quotation.

The description should include the following 15 points:

- Seller's and buyer's names and addresses
- Buyer's reference number and date of inquiry
- Listing of requested products and a brief description

- Price of each item (It is advisable to indicate whether items are new or used and to quote the price in U.S. dollars to reduce foreign exchange risk.)
- Appropriate total cubic volume and dimensions packed for export (in metric units where appropriate)
- Appropriate gross and net shipping weight (in metric units where appropriate)
- Trade discount (if applicable)
- Delivery point
- Terms of sale
- Terms of payment
- Insurance and shipping costs
- Validity period for quotation
- Total charges to be paid by customer
- Estimated shipping date from a U.S. port or airport
- Currency of sale

Pro forma invoices are not used for payment purposes. In addition to the 15 items previously mentioned, a pro forma invoice should include two statements—one that certifies the pro forma invoice is true and correct, and another that indicates the country of origin of the goods. The invoice should also be clearly marked "pro forma invoice."

Pro forma invoices are models that the buyer uses when applying for an import license, opening a letter of credit, or arranging for funds. In fact, it is a good practice to include a pro forma invoice with any international quotation, regardless of whether it has been requested. When final commercial invoices are being prepared before shipment, it is advisable to check with your local Export Assistance Center for any special invoicing provisions that may be required by the importing country.

If a specific price is agreed on or guaranteed by your company, the precise period during which the offer remains valid should be specified.

TERMS OF SALE

In any sales agreement, it is important to have a common understanding of the delivery terms because confusion over their meaning may result in a lost sale or a loss on a sale. Terms of sale define the obligations, risks, and costs of the buyer and seller involving the delivery of goods that make up the export transaction. The terms in international business transactions often sound similar to those used in domestic business, but they frequently have very different meanings. For this reason, the exporter must know and understand the terms before preparing a quotation or a pro forma invoice.

The most commonly applied terms of sale in the global marketplace are the international commercial terms, or Incoterms. A complete list of these important terms and their definitions is provided in *Incoterms 2000*, a booklet issued by the International Chamber of Commerce (ICC). To purchase the booklet, contact ICC Books, 1212 Avenue of the Americas, 18th Floor, New York, NY 10036; call (212) 703-5066; or go online.

Following are a few of the more frequently used terms in international trade:

- *CIF* stands for cost, insurance, and freight to a named overseas port. The seller quotes a price for the goods (including insurance), all transportation, and miscellaneous charges to the point of debarkation from the vessel. (The term is used only for ocean shipments.)
- *CFR* applies to cost and freight to a named overseas port. The seller quotes a price for the goods that includes the cost of transportation to the named point of debarkation from the vessel. The buyer covers the cost of insurance. (The term applies only for ocean shipments.)
- *CPT* (carriage paid to) and *CIP* (carriage and insurance paid to) apply to a named destination. These terms are used in place of CFR and CIF, respectively, for all modes of transportation, including intermodal.
- *EXW* (ex works) means "from a named point of origin" (e.g., ex factory, ex mill, ex warehouse); the price quoted applies only at the point of origin (i.e., the seller's premises). The seller agrees to place the goods at the buyer's disposal at the specified place within a fixed time period. All other obligations, risks, and costs beyond the named point of origin are the buyer's.
- *FAS,* or free alongside ship, refers to the seller's price quote for the goods, including the charge for delivery of the goods alongside a vessel at the named port of export. The seller handles the cost of wharfage, while the buyer is accountable for the costs of loading, ocean transportation, and insurance. It is the seller's responsibility to clear the goods for export. FAS, as the term implies, is used only for waterborne shipments.
- *FCA,* or free carrier, refers to a named place within the country of origin of the shipment. This term defines the seller's responsibility for handing over the goods to a named carrier at the named shipping point. According to *Incoterms 2000,* the named shipping point may be the seller's premises. In that case, it is the seller's responsibility to clear the goods for export from the United States. The term may be used for any mode of transport.
- *FOB,* or free on board, refers to a named port of export in the country of origin of the shipment. The seller quotes the buyer a price that covers all costs up to and including the loading of goods aboard a vessel. (FOB is used only for ocean shipments.) As with other "F" terms, it is the seller's responsibility to clear the goods for export.

Some of the more common terms used in chartering a vessel are as follows:

- *Free in* is a pricing term that indicates that the charterer of a vessel is responsible for the cost of loading goods onto the vessel.
- *Free in and out* is a pricing term that indicates that the charterer of the vessel is responsible for the cost of loading and unloading goods from the vessel.
- *Free out* is a pricing term that indicates that the charterer is responsible for the cost of unloading goods from the vessel.

It is important to understand and use sales terms correctly. A simple misunderstanding may prevent you from meeting contractual obligations or make you responsible for shipping costs that you sought to avoid.

When quoting a price, you should make it meaningful to the prospective buyer. For example, a price for industrial machinery quoted "EXW Saginaw, Michigan, not export packed" is meaningless to most prospective foreign buyers. The buyers might find it difficult to determine the total cost and, therefore, might hesitate to place an order. You should quote CIF or CIP prices whenever possible because such quotes show the foreign buyer the cost of getting the product to or near the desired country.

If possible, you should quote the price in U.S. dollars. This will eliminate the risk of exchange rate fluctuations and problems with currency conversion.

If you need assistance in figuring CIF or CIP prices, an international freight forwarder can help. You should furnish the freight forwarder with a description of the product to be exported and its weight and cubic measurement when packed. The freight forwarder can compute the CIF price, usually at no charge.

FACT: A common misperception of many company owners is that their prices are too high for foreign markets.

INSIGHT: What makes your product sell domestically can help it sell abroad. Price is important, but it is not the only selling point. Other competitive factors are need, utility, quality, service, credit, and consumer taste. Don't assume your price is uncompetitive. Your products could still be a bargain in countries with a strong currency, even after adding overseas delivery costs and import duties.

FACT: Pro forma invoices are the preferred method of quoting prices.

INSIGHT: It is a good practice to include a pro forma invoice with any international quotation regardless of whether it has been requested.

Chapter 14: METHODS OF PAYMENT

In This Chapter

- Different ways to receive payment when selling your products internationally
- Selection of a payment method
- Currency issues and payment problems

PRUDENT CREDIT PRACTICES

Experienced exporters extend credit cautiously. They evaluate new customers with care and continuously monitor older accounts. You may wisely decide to decline a customer's request for open-account credit if the risk is too great, and you may propose instead payment-on-delivery terms through a documentary sight draft or an irrevocable confirmed letter of credit—or even payment in advance. For a fully creditworthy customer, however, you may decide to allow a month or two for payment or perhaps even extend open-account terms.

Other good credit practices include being aware of any unfavorable changes in your customers' payment patterns, refraining from going beyond normal commercial terms, and consulting with your international banker on how to cope with unusual circumstances or in difficult markets. It is always advisable to check a buyer's credit (even if the safest payment methods are used). A U.S. Commercial Service International Company Profile (ICP) provides useful information for credit checks (see Chapter 6). For a fee, you may request an ICP on companies in many countries. The ICP contains financial background on the company and a discussion regarding its size, capitalization, years in business, and other pertinent information, such as the names of other U.S. companies that conduct business with the firm. You can then contact those U.S. companies to find out about their payment experience with the foreign firm.

Because being paid in full and on time is of the utmost concern to you, the level of risk you are willing to assume in extending credit is a major consideration. There are several ways in which you can receive payment when selling your products abroad, depending on how trustworthy you consider the buyer to be. With domestic sales, if the buyer has good credit, sales are typically made on open account; otherwise, cash in advance is required. For export sales, those are not the only common methods of payment.

Listed in order from most secure for the exporter to least secure, the basic methods of payment are:

- Cash in advance

- Documentary letter of credit
- Documentary collection or draft
- Open account
- Other payment mechanisms

CASH IN ADVANCE

Receiving payment by cash in advance of the shipment might seem ideal. In this situation, your company is relieved of collection problems and has immediate use of the money. A wire transfer is commonly used and has the advantage of being almost immediate. Payment by check may result in a collection delay of up to six weeks—perhaps defeating the original intention of receiving payment before shipment.

Many exporters accept credit cards in payment for consumer goods and other products that generally have a low dollar value and that are sold directly to the end user. Domestic and international rules governing credit card transactions sometimes differ, so U.S. merchants should contact their credit card processor for more specific information. International credit card transactions are typically handled by telephone or fax. Because those methods are subject to fraud, you should determine the validity of transactions and obtain the proper authorizations before sending goods or performing services.

For the buyer, advance payment tends to create cash flow problems and to increase risks. Furthermore, cash in advance is not as common in most of the world as it is in the United States. Buyers are often concerned that the goods may not be sent if payment is made in advance or that they will have no leverage with the seller if goods do not meet specifications. Exporters who insist on advance payment as their sole method of doing business may find themselves losing out to competitors who offer more flexible payment terms.

DOCUMENTARY LETTERS OF CREDIT AND DOCUMENTARY COLLECTIONS OR DRAFTS

Documentary letters of credit or documentary collections or drafts are often used to protect the interests of both buyer and seller. These two methods require that payment be made on presentation of documents conveying the title and showing that specific steps have been taken. Letters of credit and drafts may be paid immediately or at a later date. Drafts that are paid on presentation are called *sight drafts*. Drafts that are to be paid at a later date, often after the buyer receives the goods, are called *time drafts* or *date drafts*. A transmittal letter is used, which contains complete and precise instructions on how the documents should be handled and how the payment is to be made (see Sample Form 14.1).

Because payment by these two methods is made on the basis of documents, all terms of payment should be clearly specified in order to avoid confusion and delay. For example, "net 30 days" should be specified as "30 days from acceptance." Likewise, the currency of payment should be specified as "US$30,000." International bankers can offer other suggestions.

Banks charge fees—mainly based on a percentage of the amount of payment—for handling letters of credit and smaller amounts for handling drafts. If fees charged by both the foreign and U.S. banks are to be applied to the buyer's account, this term should be explicitly stated in all quotations and in the letter of credit.

The exporter usually expects the buyer to pay the charges for the letter of credit, but some buyers may not agree to this added cost. In such cases, you must either absorb the costs of the letter of credit or risk losing that potential sale. Letters of credit for smaller amounts can be somewhat expensive because fees can be high relative to the sale.

Letters of Credit

A letter of credit adds a bank's promise to that of the foreign buyer to pay the exporter. A letter of credit issued by a foreign bank is sometimes confirmed by a U.S. bank. This confirmation means that the U.S. bank (the confirming bank) adds its promise to that of the foreign bank (the issuing bank) to pay the exporter. If a letter of credit is not confirmed, it is "advised" through a U.S. bank and is thus called an *advised letter of credit.* U.S. exporters may wish to have letters of credit issued by foreign banks confirmed through a U.S. bank if they are unfamiliar with the foreign bank or are concerned about the political or economic risk associated with the country in which the bank is located. An Export Assistance Center or international banker can assist exporters in evaluating the risks to determine what might be appropriate for specific export transactions.

A letter of credit may be *irrevocable,* which means that it cannot be changed unless both parties agree. Alternatively, it can be *revocable,* in which case either party may unilaterally make changes. A revocable letter of credit is inadvisable because it carries many risks for the exporter.

To expedite the receipt of funds, you can use wire transfers. You should consult with your international banker about bank charges for such services.

A TYPICAL LETTER OF CREDIT TRANSACTION

Here are the typical steps in issuing an irrevocable letter of credit that has been confirmed by a U.S. bank:

1. After the exporter and the buyer agree on the terms of a sale, the buyer arranges for its bank to open a letter of credit that specifies the documents needed for payment. The buyer determines which documents will be required.

2. The buyer's bank issues, or opens, its irrevocable letter of credit and includes all instructions to the seller relating to the shipment.

3. The buyer's bank sends its irrevocable letter of credit to a U.S. bank and requests confirmation. The exporter may request that a particular U.S. bank be the confirming bank, or the foreign bank may select a U.S. correspondent bank.

4. The U.S. bank prepares a letter of confirmation to forward to the exporter along with the irrevocable letter of credit.

5. The exporter carefully reviews all conditions in the letter of credit. The exporter's freight forwarder is contacted to make sure that the shipping date can be met. If the exporter cannot comply with one or more of the conditions, the customer is alerted at once because an amendment may be necessary.

6. The exporter arranges with the freight forwarder to deliver the goods to the appropriate port or airport.

7. When the goods are loaded aboard the exporting carrier, the freight forwarder completes the necessary documentation.

8. The exporter (or the freight forwarder) presents the documents, evidencing full compliance with the letter of credit terms, to the U.S. bank.

9. The bank reviews the documents. If they are in order, the documents are sent to the buyer's bank for review and then transmitted to the buyer.

10. The buyer (or the buyer's agent) uses the documents to claim the goods.

11. A sight or time draft accompanies the letter of credit. A sight draft is paid on presentation; a time draft is paid within a specified time period.

EXAMPLE OF A CONFIRMED IRREVOCABLE LETTER OF CREDIT

Sample Form 14.2 illustrates the various parts of a typical confirmed irrevocable letter of credit. In this example, the letter of credit was forwarded to the exporter, Walton Building Supply Company, by the confirming bank, Megabank Corporation, as a result of a letter of credit issued by the Third Hong Kong Bank, Hong Kong, for the account of the importer, HHB Hong Kong. The date of issue was March 8, 2006, and the exporter must have submitted the proper documents (e.g., a commercial invoice in one original and three copies) by June 23, 2006, for a sight draft to be honored.

TIPS ON USING LETTERS OF CREDIT

When preparing quotations for prospective customers, you should keep in mind that banks pay only the amount specified in the letter of credit—even if higher charges for shipping, insurance, or other factors are incurred and documented.

On receiving a letter of credit, you should carefully compare the letter's terms with the terms of the pro forma quotation. This step is extremely important because the terms must be precisely met or the letter of credit may be invalid and you may not be paid. If meeting the terms of the letter of credit is impossible or if any of the information is incorrect or even misspelled, you should contact the customer immediately and ask for an amendment to the letter of credit.

You must provide documentation showing that the goods were shipped by the date specified in the letter of credit or you may not be paid. You should check with your freight forwarders to make sure that no unusual conditions may arise that would delay shipment.

Documents must be presented by the date specified for the letter of credit to be paid. You should verify with your international banker that there will be sufficient time to present the letter of credit documents for payment.

You may request that the letter of credit specify that partial shipments and transshipment will be allowed. Specifying what will be allowed can prevent unforeseen problems at the last minute.

Documentary Collections or Drafts

A draft, sometimes called a *bill of exchange,* is analogous to a foreign buyer's check. Like checks used in domestic commerce, drafts carry the risk that they will not be honored. However, in international commerce, title does not transfer to the buyer until the buyer pays the draft.

SIGHT DRAFTS

A sight draft is used when the exporter wishes to retain title to the shipment until it reaches its destination and payment is made. Before the shipment can be released to the buyer, the original "order" for the ocean bill of lading (the document that evidences title) must be properly endorsed by the buyer and surrendered to the carrier. It is important to note that air way bills do not need to be presented for the buyer to claim the goods. Risk increases when a sight draft is used with an air shipment.

In actual practice, the ocean bill of lading is endorsed by the exporter and sent by the exporter's bank to the buyer's bank. It is accompanied by the sight draft, invoices, and other supporting documents that are specified by either the buyer or the buyer's country (e.g., packing lists, commercial invoices, and insurance certificates). The foreign bank notifies the buyer when it has received these documents. As soon as the draft is paid, the foreign bank turns over the bill of lading, thereby enabling the buyer to obtain the shipment.

There is still some risk when a sight draft is used to control transferring the title of a shipment. The buyer's ability or willingness to pay might change between the time the goods are shipped and the time the drafts are presented for payment. There is no bank promise to pay standing behind the buyer's obligation. Also, the policies of the importing country could change. If the buyer cannot or will not pay for and claim the goods, returning or disposing of the products becomes the problem of the exporter.

Time Drafts and Date Drafts

A time draft is used when the exporter extends credit to the buyer. The draft states that payment is due by a specific time after the buyer accepts the time draft and receives the goods. By signing and writing "accepted" on the draft, the buyer is formally obligated to pay within the stated time. When this is done, the time draft is then called a *trade acceptance*. It can be kept by the exporter until maturity or sold to a bank at a discount for immediate payment.

A date draft differs slightly from a time draft in that it specifies a date on which payment is due, rather than a time period after the draft is accepted. When either a sight draft or time draft is used, a buyer can delay payment by delaying acceptance of the draft. A date draft can prevent this delay in payment, though it still must be accepted.

OPEN ACCOUNT

In a foreign transaction, an open account can be a convenient method of payment if the buyer is well established, has a long and favorable payment record, or has been thoroughly checked for creditworthiness. With an open account, the exporter simply bills the customer, who is expected to pay under agreed terms at a future date. Some of the largest firms abroad make purchases only on open account.

However, there are risks to open-account sales. The absence of documents and banking channels might make it difficult to pursue the legal enforcement of claims. The exporter might also have to pursue collection abroad, which can be difficult and costly. Another problem is that receivables may be harder to finance, because drafts or other evidence of indebtedness is unavailable. There are several ways to reduce credit risk, including export credit insurance and factoring.

Exporters contemplating a sale on open-account terms should thoroughly examine the political, economic, and commercial risks. They should also consult with their bankers if financing will be needed for the transaction before issuing a pro forma invoice to a buyer.

CONSIGNMENT SALES

International consignment sales follow the same basic procedures as in the United States. The goods are shipped to a foreign distributor, who sells them on behalf of the exporter. The exporter retains title to the goods until they are sold, at which point payment is sent to the exporter. The exporter has the greatest risk and least control over the goods with this method. Also, receiving payment may take a while.

It is smart to consider risk insurance with international consignment sales. The contract should clarify who is responsible for property risk insurance that will cover the merchandise until it is sold and payment is received. In addition, it may be necessary to conduct a credit check on the foreign distributor.

FOREIGN CURRENCY

A buyer and a seller who are in different countries rarely use the same currency. Payment is usually made in the buyer's or seller's currency or in a third mutually acceptable currency.

One of the risks associated with foreign trade is the uncertainty of future exchange rates. The relative value between the two currencies could change between the times the deal is concluded and the time payment is received. If you are not properly protected, a devaluation or depreciation of the foreign currency could cause you to lose money. For example, if the buyer has agreed to pay €500,000 for a shipment, and the euro is valued at $0.85, you would expect to receive $425,000. If the euro later decreased in value to $0.84, payment under the new rate would be only $420,000, meaning a loss of $5,000 for you. If the foreign currency increased in value, however, you would get a windfall in extra profits. Nonetheless, most exporters are not interested in speculating on foreign exchange fluctuations and prefer to avoid risks.

One of the simplest ways for you to avoid such risk is to quote prices and require payment in U.S. dollars. Then the burden of exchanging currencies and the risk are placed on the buyer. You should also be aware of any problems with currency convertibility. Not all currencies are freely or quickly converted into U.S. dollars. Fortunately, the U.S. dollar is widely accepted as an international trading currency, and U.S. firms can often secure payment in dollars.

If the buyer asks to make payment in a foreign currency, you should consult an international banker before negotiating the sales contract. Banks can offer advice on the foreign exchange risks that exist with a particular currency.

PAYMENT PROBLEMS

In international trade, problems involving bad debts are more easily avoided than rectified after they occur. Credit checks and the other methods that have been discussed in this chapter can limit the risks. Nonetheless, just as in a company's domestic business, exporters occasionally encounter problems with buyers who default on their payment. When these problems occur in international trade, obtaining payment can be both difficult and expensive. Even when the exporter has insurance to cover commercial credit risks, a default by a buyer still requires the time, effort, and cost of the exporter to collect a payment. The exporter must exercise normal business prudence in exporting and exhaust all reasonable means of obtaining payment before an insurance claim is honored. Even then, there is often a significant delay before the insurance payment is made.

The simplest and least costly solution to a payment problem is to contact and negotiate with the customer. With patience, understanding, and flexibility, you may often resolve conflicts to the satisfaction of both sides. This point is especially true when a simple misunderstanding or technical problem is to blame and there is no question of bad faith. Even though you may be required to compromise on certain points—perhaps even on the price of the committed goods—your company may save a valuable customer and profit in the long run.

However, if negotiations fail and the sum involved is large enough to warrant the effort, your company should obtain the assistance and advice of its bank, legal counsel, and the U.S. Commercial Service, which can often resolve payment problems informally. When all else fails, arbitration is often faster and less costly than legal action. The International Chamber of Commerce handles most international arbitration and is usually acceptable to foreign companies because it is not affiliated with any single country. For information, visit the Web site of the U.S. Council of the International Chamber of Commerce.

FACT: Many companies think that exporting is too risky.

INSIGHT: You can reduce risk to a safe level. Letters of credit, export credit insurance programs, and reference checks through banks and international credit reporting agencies can help protect you. Trade laws are often straightforward, and legal advice about them is easily obtained.

FACT: Credit cards are a popular method of payment for exports.

INSIGHT: Because international credit card transactions are typically handled by telephone or fax, fraud can be an issue. Determine the validity of transactions and obtain the proper authorizations before sending goods or performing services.

FACT: Some letters of credit are revocable which means that you or the buyer can unilaterally make changes. As a result, such letters of credit carry more risk than irrevocable letters of credit.

INSIGHT: Smart exporters insist on irrevocable letters of credit.

FACT: Even exporters who take precautions occasionally experience payment problems.

INSIGHT: If you experience payment problems, try these three avenues:

1. Try to negotiate directly with the customer.

2. Work with your bank, legal counsel, and the U.S. Commercial Service—particularly if negotiations fail and the sum involved is large.

3. Try arbitration through the International Chamber of Commerce if other means fail. This route is often faster and less costly than legal action.

Chapter 15: FINANCING EXPORT TRANSACTIONS

In This Chapter

- **Factors to consider in making financing decisions**
- **Private sources of financing**
- **Government sources of financing**

Export financing is often a key factor in a successful sale. Contract negotiation and closure are important, but ultimately your company must get paid. Exporters naturally want to get paid as quickly as possible, whereas importers usually prefer to delay payment until they have received or resold the goods. Because of the intense competition for export markets, being able to offer attractive payment terms is often necessary to make a sale. You should be aware of the many financing options open to you so that you choose the most acceptable one to both the buyer and your company. In many cases, government assistance in export financing for small and medium-sized businesses can increase your firm's options. The following factors are important to consider in making decisions about financing:

- **The need for financing to make the sale.** In some cases, favorable payment terms make a product more competitive. If the competition offers better terms and has a similar product, a sale can be lost. In other cases, the buyer may prefer buying from someone else but might buy your product because of shorter or more secure credit terms.
- **The length of time the product is being financed.** The term of the loan required determines how long you will have to wait before you receive payment from the buyer and influences your choice of how to finance the transaction.
- **The cost of different methods of financing.** Interest rates and fees vary, and an exporter may expect to assume some or all of the financing costs. Before submitting a pro forma invoice to the buyer, you must understand how those costs affect price and profit.
- **The risks associated with financing the transaction.** The riskier the transaction, the harder and more costly it will be to finance. The political and economic stability of the buyer's country can also be an issue. To provide financing for either accounts receivable or the production or purchase of the product for sale, the lender may require the most secure methods of payment—a letter of credit (possibly confirmed) or export credit insurance or a guarantee.

- **The need for pre-shipment financing and for post-shipment working capital.** Production for an unusually large order or for a surge of orders may present unexpected and severe strains on your working capital. Even during normal periods, inadequate working capital may curb an exporter's growth. However, assistance is available through the public and private sectors. A number of those resources are discussed in this chapter.

For help in determining which financing options may be available or the most beneficial, you may consult the following sources:

- Your banker
- Your local Department of Commerce Export Assistance Center
- Your local Small Business Administration office
- The Export-Import Bank in Washington, D.C., and selected cities
- Your state export promotion or export finance office

EXTENDING CREDIT TO FOREIGN BUYERS

Foreign buyers often press exporters for longer payment periods. Although it is true that liberal financing is a means of enhancing export competitiveness, you need to carefully weigh the credit or financing that you extend to foreign customers. Moreover, the extension of credit by the seller to the buyer is more common outside the United States. U.S. sellers who are reluctant to extend credit may face the possibility of the loss of the sale to their competitors.

A useful guide for determining the appropriate credit period is the normal commercial terms in your industry for internationally traded products. Buyers generally expect to receive the benefits of such terms. For off-the-shelf items like consumer goods, chemicals and other raw materials, agricultural commodities, and spare parts and components, normal commercial terms (with few exceptions) range from 30 to 180 days. You may have to make allowances for longer shipment times than are found in domestic trade because foreign buyers are often unwilling to have the credit period start before receiving the goods. Custom made or high-value capital equipment may warrant longer repayment periods. Once credit terms are extended to a buyer, they tend to be a precedent for future sales, so you should review with special care any credit terms extended to first-time buyers.

When exporting, your company should follow the same careful credit principles it follows for domestic customers. An important reason for controlling the credit period is the cost incurred through use of working capital or through interest and fees. If the buyer is not responsible for paying those costs, then you should factor them into the selling price. Your company should also recognize that longer credit periods may increase the risk of default. Thus, you must exercise judgment in balancing competitiveness against cost and safety. Customers are frequently charged interest on credit periods of a year or longer but less frequently on short-term credit (up to 180 days). Most exporters absorb interest charges for short-term credit unless the customer pays after the due date.

Obtaining cash immediately is usually a high priority with exporters. Converting export receivables to cash at a discount with a bank is one way to do so. Another way is to expand working capital resources. A third approach, suitable when the purchase involves capital goods and the repayment period extends a year or longer, is to arrange for third-party financing. For example, a bank could make a loan directly to the buyer for the product, and you could be paid immediately from the loan proceeds while the bank waits for payment and earns interest. A fourth possibility, when financing is difficult to obtain, is to engage in countertrade. In a countertrade, you accept goods, services, or other instruments of trade in partial or whole payment for the product. Countertrade, therefore, provides the customer with an opportunity to generate earnings to pay for the purchase.

These options may require you to pay interest, fees, or other costs. Some options are more feasible for larger amounts. Your company should also determine whether it will incur financial liability should the buyer default.

WORKING WITH COMMERCIAL BANKS

The same commercial bank services used to finance domestic activities, including revolving lines of credit for working capital, are often sought to finance export sales until payment is received. Banks do not regularly extend financing solely on the basis of an individual order; they prefer to establish an ongoing business relationship.

A logical first step if you're seeking to finance short-term export sales is to approach the local commercial bank that your company already does business with. If the bank previously has extended credit to your company, it will be familiar with your financial standing, credit need, repayment record, and ability to perform. The bank may be willing to raise the overall limit on an existing working capital line of credit, to expand its scope to cover export transactions, or to approve a separate line specifically adapted to export-related transactions that involve arrangements such as discounting.

Alternatively, you may wish to approach a commercial bank with an international department. Such a bank will be familiar with export business and will also be in a position to provide international banking services related to documentary collections and letters of credit, including the discounting of drafts. An intermediate approach is to retain a relationship with your bank but seek a referral to a correspondent bank that has an international department.

You should visit the bank's international department to discuss export plans, available banking facilities, and applicable charges. You may wish to inquire about such matters as fees for amending or confirming a letter of credit, fees for processing drafts, and the bank's experience in working with U.S. government agencies that offer export financing assistance. Generally, the bank's representative handling your account will not be located in the international department. It is in your best interest to create and foster a close working relationship with the international department.

The responsibility for repaying a working capital loan ordinarily rests with you, the seller, even if the foreign buyer fails to pay. The bank takes this contingency into account in deciding on an export working capital line of credit. Both you and the bank will benefit, though, if you improve the quality of the export receivables by using letters of credit, credit insurance, or Export-Import Bank or Small Business Administration working capital guarantees.

When shipping capital goods, you may want the commercial bank to make medium-term loans directly to the foreign buyer to finance the sale. Such loans are available for well-established foreign buyers in more stable markets. But where there is an element of risk, the bank may require a standby letter of credit, recourse to the exporter in case of default, or similar repayment reinforcement. You should be knowledgeable about loans from your own bank that are backed by Export-Import Bank guarantees and insurance—assuming that the commercial bank is willing to use them.

USING DISCOUNTING AND BANKER'S ACCEPTANCES

A time draft under an irrevocable letter of credit confirmed by a U.S. bank presents relatively little risk of default, so you may be willing to hold such a draft until it matures. Unless you have ample funds to use for other purposes, however, holding drafts will use up your working capital.

As another course of action, your bank may be willing to buy or lend against time drafts if you have a creditworthy foreign buyer who has accepted or agreed to pay at a specified future date. Such an arrangement allows you to convert the time draft into immediate cash. The amount that you receive will be less than the face value of the draft. The difference, called a *discount,* represents interest and fees that the bank charges for holding the draft until maturity. The bank may also require you to reimburse it if the draft is unpaid at the due date.

In a third option, known as a *banker's acceptance,* a commercial bank may undertake to accept the obligation of paying a draft for a fee. Banker's acceptances are usually in large denominations. Only a few well-known banks are accepted in the market as "prime name" banks for purposes of creating banker's acceptances.

USING EXPORT INTERMEDIARIES

In addition to acting as export representatives, many export intermediaries, such as export trading companies and export management companies, can help finance export sales. Export intermediaries may provide short-term financing, or they may simply purchase the goods to be exported directly from the manufacturer, thus eliminating any risks to the manufacturer that are associated with the export transaction as well as the need for financing.

USING GOVERNMENT ASSISTANCE PROGRAMS

Several federal, state, and local government agencies offer programs to assist exporters with their financing needs. Some are guarantee programs that require the participation of an approved lender; others provide loans or grants to the exporter or to a foreign government.

Government programs generally aim to improve exporters' access to credit rather than to subsidize the cost at below-market levels. With few exceptions, banks are allowed to charge market interest rates and fees, including those paid to the government agencies to cover the agencies' administrative costs and default risks. Commercial banks use government guarantee and insurance programs to reduce the risk associated with loans to exporters.

Export-Import Bank of the United States

The Export-Import Bank of the United States (Ex-Im Bank) is an independent U.S. government agency that facilitates the export of U.S. goods and services. As the federal government's export credit agency, Ex-Im Bank provides export credit insurance, loan guarantees to lenders, direct loans to exporters on market-related credit terms, and loans to foreign buyers.

Ex-Im Bank's insurance and loan guarantees are structured to encourage exporters and financial institutions to support U.S. exports by reducing t he commercial risks (such as buyer insolvency and failure to pay) and political risks (such as war and currency inconvertibility) of international trade that could result in non-payment to U.S. exporters by foreign buyers of their goods and services. The financing made available under Ex-Im Bank's guarantees and insurance is on market terms, and most of the commercial and political risks are borne by Ex-Im Bank.

Ex-Im Bank's loan program is designed to neutralize interest rate subsidies offered by foreign governments. By responding with loan assistance, Ex-Im Bank enables U.S. financing to be competitive with that offered by foreign exporters.

PREEXPORT FINANCING

The working capital guarantee enables lenders to provide the financing that an exporter needs to purchase or produce a product for export, as well as to finance short-term accounts receivable. If the exporter defaults on a loan guaranteed under this program, Ex-Im Bank reimburses the lender for the guaranteed portion—generally, 90 percent of the loan—thereby reducing the lender's overall risk. For qualified loans to minority, woman-owned, or rural businesses, Ex-Im Bank can increase its guarantee coverage to 100 percent. The working capital guarantee can be used either to support ongoing export sales or to meet a temporary need for cash flow arising from a single export transaction.

The working capital guarantee offers generous advance rates, so that exporters can increase their borrowing capacity. Those rates apply in the following categories:

- Inventory—up to 75 percent advance rate (including work-in-process—that is, material that has been released to manufacturing, engineering, design, or other services)
- Foreign accounts receivable—up to 90 percent advance rate

Guaranteed working capital loans are secured by export-related accounts receivable and inventory (including work-in-process) tied to an export order. (For letters of credit issued under a guaranteed loan, Ex-Im Bank requires collateral for only 25 percent of the value of the letter of credit.)

POSTEXPORT FINANCING

Ex-Im Bank offers export credit insurance to offset the commercial and political risks that are sometimes associated with international trade. Under the majority of policies, the insurance protects an exporter's short-term credit extended for the sale of consumer goods, raw materials, commodities, spare parts, and other items for which payment is expected within 180 days. If the buyer fails to pay, Ex-Im Bank reimburses the exporter in accordance with the terms of the policy. The majority of payment terms are up to 180 days, with some transactions qualifying for terms up to 360 days. Ex-Im Bank insurance is the largest federal program supporting short-term export credit.

Ex-Im Bank insurance policies for exporters include the Small Business Policy, the Single-Buyer Policy, and the Multi-Buyer Policy. With prior written approval, an exporter can assign the rights to any proceeds from an Ex-Im Bank insurance policy to a lender as collateral for financing. Ex-Im Bank's policies generally cover up to 100 percent of defaults caused by specified political risks, such as war and expropriation, and up to 98 percent of defaults arising from commercial risks, such as buyer default and insolvency. Exporters generally must meet U.S. content requirements and, under some policies, must insure all eligible foreign sales.

Several private companies also offer export credit insurance that covers political and commercial risks. Private insurance is available, often at competitive premium rates, to established exporters who have a proven history, although underwriting in particular markets may be limited.

Under a separate program, the bank buyer credit policy, Ex-Im Bank offers a guarantee to encourage banks and other lenders to make export loans to creditworthy foreign buyers of U.S. goods and services. Ex-Im Bank's guarantee supports either medium-term financing (1 to 5 years for repayment after delivery or equipment installation) or long-term financing (up to 10 years for repayment) for heavy equipment and capital projects, such as power plants, telecommunications systems, and transport facilities and equipment.

As an alternative to guarantees, Ex-Im Bank also offers medium- and long-term loans. Ex-Im Bank loans are made on the same terms and conditions as guarantees, with the important difference that the bank sets the interest rate in accordance with international agreements. In many cases, an Ex-Im Bank guarantee results in a cost that is lower than an Ex-ImBank loan.

Small Business Administration

The Small Business Administration (SBA) also provides financial assistance to U.S. exporters. Through its partnership with national, regional, and community lenders, SBA provides loan guarantees for export working capital and acquisition of plant and equipment, as well as capital for enabling small businesses to commence or expand export activity.

SBA's Export Working Capital Program (EWCP) will guarantee up to $1.5 million or 90 percent of the loan amount, whichever is less. These loans provide working capital for export transactions and finance export receivables. They can also support standby letters of credit used as bid or performance bonds. The loans can be set up to support individual transactions or as revolving lines of credit. Interest rates are negotiated between the borrower and the lender and may be fixed or variable.

SBA and Ex-Im Bank joined their working capital programs to offer a unified approach to the government's support of export financing. The EWCP uses a one-page application form and streamlined documentation. Turnaround is usually in 10 days or less. A letter of prequalification is also available from SBA.

If a larger loan guarantee is needed, Ex-Im Bank has a similar loan program to handle loan amounts in the multimillion dollar range.

Under its International Trade Loan Program, SBA can guarantee up to $1.25 million in combined working capital loans and loans for facilities and equipment (including land and buildings; construction of new facilities; renovation, improvement, or expansion of existing facilities; and purchase or reconditioning of machinery, equipment, and fixtures). Applicants must either (a) certify that loan proceeds will enable them to significantly expand existing export markets or develop new ones or (b) show that they have been adversely affected by import competition. Interest rates are negotiated between the small business exporter and the lender.

Export Express is a program that expedites multipurpose loans for small businesses. The Small Business Administration delegates the authority to approved lenders to unilaterally approve SBA-guaranteed loans. The lenders can use their own forms and can usually approve applications within a week. Export Express loans have a cap of $250,000. Loans of up to $150,000 receive an 85 percent SBA guarantee, and loans over that amount receive a 75 percent SBA guarantee. To be eligible, a business must have been in operation for at least one year and must show that it will enter into or increase its export sales as a result of the loan. SBA's other eligibility requirements also apply. Eligible use of proceeds includes financing of export development activities, transaction-specific financing for export orders, revolving export lines of credit, fixed asset loans, and financing of standby letters of credit used as bid and performance bonds.

The EWCP, the International Trade Loan Program, and Export Express all require the participation of an eligible commercial bank. Most bankers are familiar with SBA's guarantee programs, but you should ask to speak to the SBA division of the lender you approach.

In addition to these export-oriented programs, SBA offers a variety of other loan programs that may meet specific needs of small businesses. For example, SBA's Surety Bond Program may help small exporters obtain bid or performance bonds that are required on construction contracts and on many service and supply contracts. Bid and performance bonds may be required when a small U.S. company is bidding on a contract with a foreign government or with a foreign prime contractor.

Department of Agriculture

The Foreign Agricultural Service (FAS) of the U.S. Department of Agriculture (USDA) provides several programs to assist in the financing of exports of U.S. agricultural goods.

The USDA's Commodity Credit Corporation (CCC) administers export credit guarantees for commercial financing of U.S. agricultural exports. The guarantees encourage exports to buyers in countries where credit is necessary to maintain or increase U.S. sales but where financing may not be available without CCC guarantees.

The Export Credit Guarantee Program (GSM-102) covers credit terms up to three years. GSM-102 underwrites credit extended by the private banking sector in the United States (or, less commonly, by the U.S. exporter) to approved foreign banks using dollar-denominated, irrevocable letters of credit to pay for food and agricultural products sold to foreign buyers.

The Supplier Credit Guarantee Program (SCGP) is designed to make it easier for exporters to sell U.S. food products overseas by insuring short-term, open-account financing. Under the security of the SCGP, U.S. exporters become more competitive by extending longer credit terms or increasing the amount of credit available to foreign buyers without increasing financial risk. Foreign buyers benefit because they can increase their purchasing power and profit opportunities and can gain significant cash flow management advantages.

The Facility Guarantee Program (FGP) provides payment guarantees to facilitate the financing of manufactured goods and services exported from the United States to improve or establish agriculture-related facilities in emerging markets. By supporting such facilities, the FGP is designed to enhance sales of U.S. agricultural commodities and products to emerging markets, where the demand for such commodities and products may be constricted because of inadequate storage, processing, or handling capabilities for such products.

The FAS maintains a Web site to expedite and simplify applications to these financing programs. The General Sales Manager (GSM) Online System enables U.S. exporters and U.S. banks to submit required documentation electronically for the GSM-102, SCGP, and FGP.

Exporters who need further information should contact the Contract and Registration Branch of the FAS at (202) 720-3224 or by e-mail at *AskGSM@fas.usda.gov*. U.S. banks needing further information should contact the Bank Analysis Branch of FAS at (202) 690-1249.

Overseas Private Investment Corporation

The Overseas Private Investment Corporation (OPIC) is a federal agency that facilitates U.S. foreign direct investment in developing nations and emerging market economies. OPIC is an independent, financially self-supporting corporation that is fully owned by the U.S. government.

OPIC encourages U.S. investment projects overseas by offering political risk insurance, all-risk guarantees, and direct loans. OPIC political risk insurance protects U.S. investment ventures abroad against the risks of civil strife and other violence, expropriation, and inconvertibility of currency. In addition, OPIC can cover business income loss caused by political violence or expropriation.

OPIC can offer up to $400 million in total project support for any one project—up to $250 million in project financing and up to $250 million in political risk insurance. The amount of insurance and financing available to projects in the oil and gas sector with offshore, hard-currency revenues is $300 million per product and $400 million if the project receives a credit evaluation of investment grade or higher from major ratings agencies. However, the maximum support OPIC may offer an individual project is $400 million, either by combined or single OPIC products.

U.S. exporters often can benefit from the construction and equipping of new facilities financed by OPIC, although the recipients of OPIC transactions are U.S. investors. U.S. exporters and contractors operating abroad can benefit directly from an OPIC program covering wrongful calling of bid, performance, advance payment, or other guarantees. Under another program, OPIC ensures against expropriation of construction equipment temporarily located abroad, spare parts warehoused abroad, and some cross-border operating and capital loans.

OPIC also provides services to facilitate wider participation by smaller U.S. businesses in overseas investment. They include investment missions, a computerized data bank, and investor information services. OPIC has undertaken several initiatives to increase its support for U.S. small businesses in their efforts to invest in emerging markets overseas. The Small and Medium Enterprise Department and OPIC's Small Business Center were established specifically to address the needs of small and medium-sized American companies and to ease their entry into new markets. A small business insurance "wrap" is offered to companies undertaking projects through the Small Business Center. A partnership with SBA enhances OPIC's outreach to the small business community.

OBTAINING FUNDING FROM MULTILATERAL DEVELOPMENT BANKS

Multilateral development banks (MDBs) are international financial institutions owned by member governments. Their individual and collective objective is to promote economic and social progress in their developing member countries. The MDBs consist of the African Development Bank, the Asian Development Bank, the European Bank for Reconstruction and Development, the Inter-American Development Bank, and the World Bank Group. They achieve their objective by providing loans, technical cooperation, grants, capital investment, and other types of assistance to governments, government agencies, and other entities in their developing member countries. The practical expression of MDB support usually takes the form of a project or study.

Increasingly, the MDBs are providing funding to private-sector entities for private projects in developing countries. A growing number of companies and project developers around the world are taking advantage of this funding, which is secured on the basis of the financial, economic, and social viability of the projects in question.

The MDBs have traditionally been heavily involved in infrastructure and poverty alleviation projects. All the banks support projects in the following areas: agriculture, energy, environment, finance, industry, transportation, telecommunications, health, education, urban development, tourism, microenterprises, and the public sector, as well as other types of economic reform. All the banks provide some funding for private ventures, too.

The MDBs also provide debt, equity, and guarantee financing to eligible private ventures in developing countries. These funds, offered on commercial terms, can be accessed directly by private project sponsors and do not require a government guarantee.

U.S. companies receive less business from the banks than do businesses from other developed countries because fewer U.S. companies compete for the banks' business. Substantial export opportunities are available to U.S. companies, and to increase U.S. business participation, the Department of Commerce maintains liaison offices at the MDBs.

EXPLORING STATE AND LOCAL EXPORT FINANCE PROGRAMS

Several cities and states have funded and operate export financing programs, including pre-shipment and post-shipment working capital loans and guarantees, accounts receivable financing, and export insurance. To be eligible for these programs, an export sale must generally be made under a letter of credit or with credit insurance coverage. A certain percentage of state or local content may also be required. However, some programs may require only that certain facilities, such as a state or local port, be used.

To explore these and other options for financing, contact a U.S. Commercial Service Export Assistance Center. You may also contact your state's economic development agency.

FACT: Owners of small businesses often believe that they can't afford to export.

INSIGHT: Recognizing the special needs of small firms, several federal agencies have taken major steps to help small and medium-sized businesses access capital to support their export activities. The agencies include the Small Business Administration, the Export-Import Bank, and the Overseas Private Investment Corporation.

Chapter 16: BUSINESS TRAVEL ABROAD

In This Chapter

- Documents you need to travel internationally
- Tips for travel and business meetings in your destination country
- Cultural factors to take into account

It is important to visit overseas markets—before any transaction occurs. Many foreign markets differ greatly from the domestic market, and by visiting another country you can familiarize yourself with cultural nuances that may affect the design, packaging, or advertising of your product. Traveling abroad can generate new customers. As in the United States, clients and customers overseas often prefer to conduct business in person before concluding a transaction.

A successful business trip typically requires substantial. This chapter focuses on the many steps you need to take before traveling abroad and offers recommendations that will make the trip more successful.

OBTAINING PROPER DOCUMENTATION

All overseas travelers are required to have proper documentation before leaving the United States. You must have a current U.S. passport, visas from certain host countries, and—in some instances—vaccination records. If you're bringing a product for demonstration or sample purposes, an ATA carnet may also be helpful. Businesses should allow six to eight weeks to acquire all the necessary documents.

Carnets

The ATA carnet is a standardized international customs document used to obtain duty-free temporary admission of certain goods. The abbreviation ATA is derived from the French words *admission temporaire* and the English words *temporary admission*. Countries that are signatories to the ATA Convention require the carnet. Under the ATA Convention, commercial and professional travelers may temporarily take commercial samples; tools of the trade; advertising material; and cinematographic, audiovisual, medical, scientific, or other professional equipment into member countries without paying customs duties and taxes or posting a bond at the border of each country to be visited.

You should contact the U.S. Council for International Business to determine if the country you are visiting is a member of the ATA Convention. Carnets are generally valid for 12 months. To receive an application or to ask questions, contact the U.S. Council for International Business, 1212 Avenue of the Americas, New York, NY 10036; call (866) 786-5625.

Passports

All travel outside the United States and its possessions requires a valid U.S. passport. Information is available from the nearest local passport office. A wealth of information is available online from the U.S. Department of State about U.S. passports, applications, and renewals. You can obtain a nationwide listing of government offices that have passport applications, or you can download a printable application from the State Department.

Visas

Many countries require visas, but they cannot be obtained through the Passport Services Directorate. Visas are provided by a foreign country's embassy or consulate in the United States for a small fee. You must have a current U.S. passport to obtain a visa, and in many cases, a recent photo is required. You should allow several weeks to obtain visas, especially if you are traveling to developing nations. Some foreign countries require visas for business travel but not for tourist travel. When you request visas from a consulate or an embassy, you should notify the authorities that you will be conducting business. You should check visa requirements each time you travel to a country because regulations change periodically. Contact an Export Assistance Center to learn about documentation requirements for the countries where you will be traveling.

Vaccinations

Requirements for vaccinations differ by country. Although there may not be any restrictions on direct travel to and from the United States, there may be restrictions if you travel indirectly and stop over in another country before reaching your final destination. Vaccinations against typhus, typhoid, and other diseases are advisable even though they are not required. The Centers for Disease Control and Prevention (CDC) maintains a Web page to advise travelers of current conditions by country and region.

Foreign Customs

Because foreign customs regulations vary by country, you are advised to learn in advance the regulations that apply to each country that you will be visiting. If allowances for cigarettes, liquor, currency, and certain other items are not taken into account, those items can be impounded at national borders.

PLANNING AN ITINERARY

Travel agents can arrange transportation and hotel reservations quickly and efficiently. They can also help plan the itinerary, obtain the best travel rates, explain which countries require visas, advise on hotel rates and locations, and provide other valuable services. Because hotels, airlines, and other carriers pay travel agents' fees, this assistance and expertise may be free.

A well-planned itinerary enables you to make the best use of your time abroad. Although it is expensive to travel and your time is valuable, an overloaded schedule can be counterproductive. Two or three definite appointments, confirmed well in advance and spaced comfortably throughout a day, are more productive and enjoyable than a crowded agenda that forces you to rush from one meeting to the next before business is really concluded. If possible, you should plan an extra day to rest to deal with jet lag before starting your scheduled business appointments. As you plan your trip, you should keep the following travel tips in mind:

- The travel plans should reflect your company's goals and priorities.
- You should obtain the names of possible contacts, arrange appointments, and check transportation schedules before the trip begins. The most important meetings should be confirmed before you leave the United States. The U.S. Commercial Service can offer assistance through programs such as the Gold Key Service. Refer to Chapter 6 for additional information.
- As a rule, you should keep the schedule flexible enough to allow for both unexpected problems (such as transportation delays) and unexpected opportunities. For instance, accepting an unscheduled luncheon invitation from a prospective client should not keep you from missing the next scheduled meeting.
- You should confirm the normal workdays and business hours in the countries being visited. In many Middle Eastern countries, for instance, the workweek typically runs from Saturday to Thursday. Lunchtimes of two to four hours are customary in many countries.
- You should also contact an Export Assistance Center to learn of any travel advisories issued by the U.S. Department of State for countries you plan to visit. Advisories alert travelers to potentially dangerous in-country situations. The U.S. Department of State also includes travel advisories on its Web site.

OBTAINING ASSISTANCE FROM U.S. EMBASSIES AND CONSULATES

When planning a trip, you can discuss your needs and the services available at particular embassies with the staff of your local Export Assistance Center. You may also find it useful to read the appropriate Country Commercial Guide provided by the Department of Commerce.

Commercial and economic officers in U.S. embassies and consulates abroad assist U.S. exporters by providing in-depth briefings and arranging introductions to appropriate firms, individuals, or foreign government officials. Your local Export Assistance Center can help you access these services, or you can contact embassy and consulate personnel directly. Arrangements should be made as far ahead as possible. You may also find it useful to read the appropriate Country Commercial Guide provided by the Department of Commerce.

Also, a description of your firm and the extent of your international experience would be helpful to U.S. government officials abroad. Addresses of U.S. embassies and consulates throughout the world are available on the U.S. State Department Web site.

CONSIDERING CULTURAL FACTORS

Businesspeople who hope to profit from their travel should learn about the history, culture, and customs of the countries they wish to visit. Flexibility and cultural adaptation should be the guiding principles for traveling abroad on business. Business manners and methods, religious customs, dietary practices, humor, and acceptable dress vary from country to country. You can prepare for your overseas visits by reading travel guides, which are located in the travel sections of most libraries and bookstores.

Some of the cultural differences that U.S. firms most often face involve business styles, attitudes toward business relationships and punctuality, negotiating styles, gift-giving customs, greetings, significance of gestures, meanings of colors and numbers, and customs regarding titles.

The cultural anthropology literature has given us many insights into how other countries do business and how to avoid cultural blunders. One example is that Thais consider it a serious offense for someone to touch them on the head. Useful to know? Maybe. But it's hard to imagine in the United States or anywhere else businesspeople meeting for the first time or even after several times and engaging in head touching or hair messing. So by all means read the literature and talk with people who know the culture. But don't be intimidated and don't be reluctant to meet people. And do keep these general rules in mind.

Understanding and heeding cultural differences are critical to success in international business. Lack of familiarity with the business practices, social customs, and etiquette of a country can weaken your company's position in the market, prevent you from accomplishing your objectives, and ultimately lead to the failure of your exporting effort.

Americans must pay close attention to different styles of doing business and the degree of importance placed on developing business relationships. In some countries, businesspeople have a very direct style, while in others they are more subtle and value personal relationships more than most U.S. businesspeople do. For example, in the Middle East, engaging in small talk before engaging in business is standard practice.

Attitudes toward punctuality vary greatly from one culture to another, and misunderstanding those attitudes may cause confusion. Romanians, Japanese, and Germans are very punctual, whereas people in many of the Latin countries have a more relaxed attitude toward time. The Japanese consider it rude to be late for a business meeting but acceptable—even fashionable—to be late for a social occasion. In Guatemala, though, one might arrive from 10 minutes early to 45 minutes late for a luncheon appointment.

When cultural lines are being crossed, something as simple as a greeting can be misunderstood. Traditional greetings include shaking hands, hugging, kissing, and placing the hands in praying position. The "wrong" greeting can lead to an awkward encounter.

People around the world use body movements and gestures to convey specific messages. Misunderstandings over gestures are common occurrences in intercultural communication and can lead to business complications and social embarrassment.

Proper use of names and titles is often a source of confusion in international business relations. In many countries (including Denmark, France, and the United Kingdom), it is appropriate to use titles until use of first names is suggested. First names are seldom used when doing business in Germany. Visiting businesspeople should use the surname preceded by the title. Titles such as "Herr Direktor" are sometimes used to indicate prestige, status, and rank. Thais, however, address one another by first names and reserve last names for very formal occasions and written communications. In Belgium, it is important to address French-speaking business contacts as "Monsieur" or "Madame," whereas Flemish-speaking contacts should be addressed as "Mr." or "Mrs." To confuse the two is a great insult.

Understanding the customs concerning gift giving is also important. In some cultures, gifts are expected, and failure to present them is considered an insult. In other countries, though, offering a gift is considered offensive. Business executives also need to know when to present a gift (on the initial visit or afterward, for instance); where to present the gift (in public or private, for example); what type of gift to present; what color it should be; and how many gifts to present.

Gift giving is an important part of doing business in Japan, where gifts are usually exchanged at the first meeting. In sharp contrast, gifts are rarely exchanged in Germany and are usually not appropriate. Gift giving is not a usual custom in Belgium or the United Kingdom either, although in both countries, flowers are a suitable gift when you are invited to someone's home.

Customs concerning the exchange of business cards also vary. Although this point may seem of minor importance, card giving is a key part of business protocol. In Japan, for example, the Western practice of accepting a business card and pocketing it immediately is considered rude. The proper approach is to carefully look at the card after accepting it, observe the title and organization, acknowledge with a nod that the information has been digested, and perhaps make a relevant comment or ask a polite question.

Negotiating is a complex process even between parties from the same nation. It is even more complicated in international transactions because of the potential misunderstandings that stem from cultural differences. It is essential to understand the importance of rank in the other country and to know who the decision-makers are. It is important to be familiar with the business style of the foreign company, to understand the nature of agreements there, and to know the significance of gestures and negotiating etiquette.

Through research or training, you can have a working knowledge of the business culture, management attitudes, business methods, and consumer habits before you travel abroad. That knowledge is very likely to have a positive effect on your overseas travel. Your local Export Assistance Center can provide what you need to make a strong first impression.

FACT: Gathering and generating the proper documentation or overseas business travel requires time and attention to detail.

INSIGHT: Allow six to eight weeks to acquire all the documents.

FACT: First impressions are important.

INSIGHT: Americans must pay attention to different styles of doing business. In some countries, businesspeople have a very direct style, while in others they are more subtle and place more value on personal relationships.

Chapter 17: SELLING OVERSEAS AND AFTER-SALES SERVICE

In This Chapter

- Establishing a policy to deal with international inquiries
- Researching an international company before conducting business
- Building and maintaining a working relationship with an overseas customer
- Reviewing options for service delivery to foreign buyers

Many successful exporters first started selling internationally by responding to an inquiry from a foreign firm. Thousands of U.S. firms receive such requests annually, but most firms do not become successful exporters. Generally, successful firms make it a priority to create systems to properly respond to inquiries, conduct research on foreign customers, differentiate between domestic and international sales, and build positive relationships with partners.

RESPONDING TO INQUIRIES

Most, but not all, foreign letters, faxes, or e-mails of inquiry are in English. Your firm may look to certain service providers (such as banks or freight forwarders) for assistance in translating a letter of inquiry in a foreign language. Colleges and universities are also excellent sources for translation services. Most large cities have commercial translators who are hired for a fee.

A foreign firm will typically request product specifications, information, and a price. Some inquiries will come directly from the end user, whereas other inquiries will come from distributors and agents who wish to sell the product in their market. A few foreign firms may already be familiar with your product and may wish to place an order immediately.

Regardless of the form such inquiries take; your firm should establish a policy to deal with them. Here are a few suggestions:

- Expect some inquiries to have grammatical or typographical errors because the writer may know English only as a second language.
- Reply promptly, completely, and clearly. The correspondent naturally wants to know something about your firm before a transaction takes place. The reply should introduce your firm sufficiently and establish it as a reliable supplier. The reply should provide a short but adequate introduction to the firm, including bank

references and other sources that confirm reliability. Your firm's policy on exports should be stated, including cost, terms, and delivery. Your firm may wish to respond with a pro forma invoice (see Chapter 13).
- Enclose information on your firm's goods or services.
- If the company needs to meet a deadline, send the information by e-mail or fax. Unlike telephone communications, these methods may be used effectively despite differences in time zones and languages.
- Keep a record of foreign inquiries. They may turn into definite prospects as your export business grows. If your firm has an intermediary handling exports, the intermediary may use the information.

LEARNING ABOUT POTENTIAL CLIENTS

There are many ways for a U.S. firm to research a foreign company before conducting any formal business. Your company can save time and money by using the following resources:

- **Business libraries.** Several private-sector publications list and qualify international firms. There are also many directories devoted to specific regions and countries.
- **International banks.** Bankers have access to vast amounts of information on foreign firms and are usually very willing to assist corporate customers.
- **Foreign embassies.** Foreign embassies are located in Washington, D.C., and some have consulates in other major cities. The commercial (business) sections of most foreign embassies have directories of firms located in their countries.
- **Sources of credit information.** Credit reports on foreign companies are available from many private-sector sources and from the U.S. Commercial Service. For help in identifying sources of credit reports, contact your nearest Export Assistance Center.
- **Commercial Service overseas offices.** Commercial Service officers can prepare International Company Profiles or help with background reports on foreign firms.

CONDUCTING BUSINESS INTERNATIONALLY

Companies should be aware of basic business practices that are essential to successful international selling. Because cultures vary, there is no single business code. The following basic practices transcend culture barriers, though, and will help your company conduct business overseas.

- **Keep promises.** The biggest complaint from foreign importers about U.S. suppliers is failure to ship as promised. A first order is particularly important because it shapes the customer's image of a firm as a dependable or an undependable supplier.
- **Be polite, courteous, and friendly.** It is important to avoid undue familiarity or slang, which may be misinterpreted. Some overseas firms feel that the usual brief U.S. business letter is lacking in courtesy.
- **Personally sign all letters.** Form letters are not satisfactory.

BUILDING A WORKING RELATIONSHIP

Once you have established a relationship with an overseas customer, representative, or distributor, it is important to work on building and maintaining that relationship. Common courtesy should dictate business activity. By following the points outlined in this chapter, your firm can present itself well. Beyond these points, you should keep in mind that a foreign contact should be treated and served as well as a domestic contact. For example, your company should keep customers and contacts notified of all changes, including changes in price, personnel, address, and phone numbers.

Because of distance, a contact can "age" quickly and cease to be useful unless communication is maintained. If your firm cannot afford frequent travel, you may use fax, e-mail, and telephone to keep the working relationship active and up to date.

PROVIDING AFTER-SALES SERVICE

Quality, price, and service are three factors critical to the success of any export sales effort. Quality and price are addressed in earlier chapters. Service, which is addressed here, should be an integral part of any company's export strategy from the start. Properly handled, service can be a foundation for growth. Ignored or left to chance, it can cause an export effort to fail.

Service is the prompt delivery of the product. It is courteous sales personnel. It is a user or service manual modified to meet your customer's needs. It is ready access to a service facility. It is knowledgeable, cost-effective maintenance, repair, or replacement. Service is location. Service is dealer support.

Service varies by the product type, the quality of the product, the price of the product, and the distribution channel used. For certain export products—such as food products, some consumer goods, and commercial disposables—service ends once distribution channels, quality criteria, and return policies have been identified.

However, the characteristics of consumer durables and some consumables demand that service be available after the purchase is completed. For such products, service is a feature expected by the consumer. In fact, foreign buyers of industrial goods typically place service at the forefront of the criteria they evaluate when making a decision about a purchase.

All foreign markets are sophisticated, and each has its own expectations of suppliers and vendors. U.S. manufacturers or distributors must therefore ensure that their service performance is comparable to that of the predominant competitors in the market. This level of performance is an important determinant in ensuring a competitive position, especially if the other factors of product quality, price, promotion, and delivery appeal to the buyer.

You may decide, as part of your exporting strategy, not to provide after-sales service. Your company may determine that its export objective is the single or multiple opportunistic entries into export markets. Although this approach may work in the short term, your subsequent product offerings will be less successful as buyers recall the failure to provide expected levels of service. As a result, market development and sales expenditures may result in one-time sales.

Reviewing Service Delivery Options

Service is an important factor in the initial export sale and ongoing success of products in foreign markets. Your firm has many options for the delivery of service to foreign buyers.

REQUIRING THE BUYER TO RETURN THE PRODUCT

A high-cost option—and the most inconvenient for the foreign retail, wholesale, commercial, or industrial buyer—is for the product to be returned to the manufacturing or distribution facility in the United States for service or repair. The buyer incurs a high cost and loses the use of the product for an extended period, while you must incur the export cost of the same product a second time to return it. Fortunately, there are practical, cost-effective alternatives to this approach.

USING A LOCAL PARTNER

For goods sold at retail outlets, a preferred service option is to identify and use local service facilities. Although this approach requires upfront expenses to identify and train the staff for local service outlets, the costs are more than repaid in the long run.

Exporting a product into commercial or industrial markets may dictate a different approach. For the many U.S. companies that sell through distributors, selection of a representative to serve a region, a nation, or a market should be based not only on the distributing company's ability to sell effectively but also on its ability and willingness to service the product.

Assessing that ability to provide service requires that you ask questions about existing service facilities; about the types, models, and age of existing service equipment; about training practices for service personnel; and about the firm's experience in servicing similar products.

If the selected export distribution channel is a joint venture or other partnership arrangement, the overseas partner may have a service or repair capability in the markets to be penetrated. Your firm's negotiations and agreements with its partner should include explicit provisions for repairs, maintenance, and warranty service. The cost of providing this service should be negotiated into the agreement.

If the product being exported is to be sold directly to end users, service and timely performance are critical to success. The nature of the product may require delivery of on-site service to the buyer within a very specific time period. You must be prepared to negotiate such issues. On-site service may be available from service organizations in the buyer's country, or your company may have to send personnel to the site to provide service. The sales contract should anticipate a reasonable level of on-site service and should include the associated costs. Existing performance and service history can serve as a guide for estimating service and warranty requirements on export sales. This practice is accepted by small and large exporters alike.

If your export activity in a particular region grows to a considerable level, it may become cost-effective for your company to establish its own branch or subsidiary operation in the foreign market. The branch or subsidiary may be a one-person operation or a more extensive facility staffed with sales, administrative, service, and other personnel, most of whom are local nationals. This high-cost option enables you to ensure sales and service quality, provided that personnel are trained in sales, products, and service on an ongoing basis. A benefit of this option is the control it gives you and the ability to serve multiple markets in a single region.

If you have neither partners nor joint venture arrangements in a foreign market, you must be prepared to accept return of merchandise that the foreign buyer refuses to take. This situation is not likely to occur in cash-in-advance or confirmed letter of credit transactions. However, in an open-account or documentary collection transaction, the buyer is in a position to refuse delivery of the goods and suffer no financial harm. If you cannot find another buyer in that market or if you elect not to abandon the goods, you will be faced with the fees and charges associated with returning the goods to the United States. Your freight forwarder can be of great assistance in this process should the need arise and can quote you a price to return the goods.

Considering Legal Options

Service is an important part of many types of representative agreements. For better or worse, the quality of service in a country or region affects your company's reputation there.

It is imperative that agreements with a representative be specific about the form of the repair or service facility, the number of people on the staff, inspection provisions, training programs, and payment of costs associated with maintaining a suitable facility. The depth or breadth of a warranty in a given country or region should be tied to the service facility that you have access to in that market. It is important to promise only what you can deliver.

Another part of the representative agreement may detail the training you will provide to your foreign representative. Such detail may include how often training will be provided, who must be trained, where training will be provided, and which party will absorb travel and per diem costs.

Taking Advantage of New Sales Opportunities and Improved Customer Relations

Foreign buyers of U.S.-manufactured products typically have limited contact with the manufacturer or its personnel. The Foreign Service facility is one of the major contact points between you and the buyer. To a great extent, your reputation is made by the overseas service facility.

Each foreign market offers a unique opportunity for your company. Care and attention to the development of in-country sales and distribution capabilities are paramount. Delivery of after-sales service is critical to the short- and long-term success of your company's efforts in any market.

Senior personnel from your company should commit to a program of regular travel to each foreign market to meet with representatives, clients, and others who are important to the success of your firm in that market. Among those people would be the commercial officer at the Commercial Service's post and representatives of the American Chamber of Commerce and the local chamber of commerce or business association.

The benefits of such a program are twofold. First, executive management learns more about the foreign marketplace and the foreign service facility's capabilities. Second, your customer will appreciate the attention and understand the importance of the foreign market in your company's long-term plans. As a result, such visits will help you build a continuing productive relationship with your overseas clients.

FACT: Rather than engage in direct marketing, most small exporters simply take orders from abroad.

INSIGHT: Be prepared. Establish a policy to deal with inquiries from abroad:

- Consider the possible need for translation services.
- Know how to research a foreign company before conducting any formal business.
- Promptly reply to all inquiries.
- Know the basic business practices that are key to successful selling in the target market.
- Create a database of foreign inquiries.

FACT: Properly handled, service can be a foundation for growth. Ignored or left to chance, it can cause an export to fail.

INSIGHT: You have many options for handling your after-sales service:

- Have the product returned to the United States for service or repair.
- Identify and use local service facilities.
- Provide on-site service.
- Create a branch or subsidiary to provide service in the country.
- Be prepared to accept return of merchandise if the foreign buyer refuses to accept it.

Appendix: Glossary

Air waybill: Bill of lading that covers both domestic and international flights transporting goods to a specified destination. It is a non-negotiable instrument of air transport that serves as a receipt for the shipper, indicating that the carrier has accepted the goods listed therein, and obligates the carrier to carry the consignment to the airport of destination according to specified conditions.

Antidiversion clause: To help ensure that U.S. exports go only to legally authorized destinations, the U.S. government requires a destination control statement on shipping documents. Under this requirement, the commercial invoice and bill of lading (or air waybill) for nearly all commercial shipments leaving the United States must display a statement notifying the carrier and all foreign parties that the U.S. material has been approved for export only to certain destinations and may not be diverted contrary to U.S. law.

Antidumping duty: Special duty imposed to offset the price effect of dumping that has been determined to be materially harmful to domestic producers. (See also *dumping*.)

Arbitration: Process of resolving a dispute or a grievance outside of the court system by presenting it to an impartial third party or panel for a decision that may or may not be binding.

Bill of lading: Contract between the owner of the goods and the carrier. For vessels, there are two types: a straight bill of lading, which is not negotiable, and a negotiable, or shipper's orders, bill of lading. The latter can be bought, sold, or traded while the goods are in transit.

Carnet: Standardized international customs document known as an ATA (*admission temporaire* or *temporary admission*) carnet that is used to obtain duty-free temporary admission of certain goods into the countries that are signatories to the ATA Convention. Under the ATA Convention, commercial and professional travelers may take commercial samples; tools of the trade; advertising material; or cinematographic, audiovisual, medical, scientific, or other professional equipment into member countries temporarily without paying customs duties and taxes or posting a bond at the border of each country to be visited.

Cash in advance (advance payment): Payment from a foreign customer to a U.S. exporter prior to actually receiving the exporter's products. It is the least risky form of payment from the exporter's perspective.

Certificate of origin: Signed statement required in certain nations attesting to the origin of the export item. Certificates of origin are usually validated by a semiofficial organization, such as a local chamber of commerce. A North American Free Trade Agreement (NAFTA) certificate of origin is required for products traded among the NAFTA countries (Canada, Mexico, and the United States) when duty preference is claimed for NAFTA qualified goods.

CFR: Cost and freight to a named overseas port.

CIF: Cost, insurance, and freight to a named overseas post. The seller quotes a price for the goods shipped by ocean (including insurance), all transportation costs, and miscellaneous charges to the point of debarkation from the vessel.

CIP: Carriage and insurance paid for delivery to a named destination.

Commercial invoice: Document prepared by the exporter or freight forwarder and required by the foreign buyer to prove ownership and to arrange for payment to the exporter. It should provide basic information about the transaction, including a description of goods, the address of the shipper and seller, and the delivery and payment terms. In most cases, the commercial invoice is used to assess customs duties.

Confirming house: Company, based in a foreign country, that acts as a foreign buyer's agent and places confirmed orders with U.S. exporters. The confirming house guarantees payment to the exporters.

Consignment: Delivery of merchandise to the buyer or distributor, whereby the latter agrees to sell it and only then pay the U.S. exporter. The seller retains ownership of the goods until they are sold but also carries all of the financial burden and risk.

Consular invoice: Document required in some countries that describes the shipment of goods and shows information such as the consignor, consignee, and value of the shipment. Certified by the consular official of the foreign country stationed in the United States, it is used by the country's customs officials to verify the value, quantity, and nature of the shipment.

Contract: Written or oral agreement that is legally enforceable.

Copyright: Protection granted to the authors and creators of literary, artistic, dramatic, and musical works, sound recordings, and certain other intellectual works. A computer program, for example, is considered a literary work in the United States and some other countries.

Countertrade: General expression meaning the sale or barter of goods on a reciprocal basis. There may also be multilateral transactions involved.

Countervailing duties: Additional duties imposed by an importing country to offset government subsidies in an exporting country when the subsidized imports cause material injury to domestic industry in the importing country.

CPT: Carriage paid to a named destination. This term is used in place of CFR and CIF for all modes of transportation, including intermodal.

Customs-bonded warehouse: Building or other secured area in which dutiable goods may be stored, may be manipulated, or may undergo manufacturing operations without payment of duty.

Customs declaration: Document that traditionally accompanies exported goods bearing such information as the nature of the goods, their value, the consignee, and their ultimate destination. Required for statistical purposes, it accompanies all controlled goods being exported under the appropriate permit.

Customs invoice: Document used to clear goods through customs in the importing country by providing evidence of the value of goods. In some cases, the commercial invoice may be used for this purpose.

Date draft: Document used when the exporter extends credit to the buyer. It specifies a date on which payment is due, rather than a time period as with the time draft.

Direct exporting: Sale by an exporter directly to an importer located in another country.

Distributor: Merchant in the foreign country who purchases goods from the U.S. exporter (often at a discount) and resells them for a profit. The foreign distributor generally provides support and service for the product, relieving the U.S. exporter of these responsibilities.

Dock receipt: Receipt issued by an ocean carrier to acknowledge receipt of a shipment at the carrier's dock or warehouse facilities.

Documentary letter of credit or documentary draft: Document used to protect the interests of both buyer and seller. A letter of credit requires that payment be made on the basis of the presentation of documents to a lender conveying the title and indicating that specific steps have been taken. Letters of credit and drafts may be paid immediately or at a later date. Drafts that are paid on presentation are called *sight drafts*. Drafts that are to be paid at a later date, often after the buyer receives the goods, are called *time drafts* or *date drafts*.

Dumping: Sale of an imported commodity at a price lower than the cost of production in the exporting country. Dumping is considered an actionable trade practice when it disrupts markets and injures producers of competitive products in the importing country. Article VI of the General Agreement on Tariffs and Trade (World Trade Organization) permits the imposition of special antidumping duties on goods equal to the difference between their export price and their normal value.

E-commerce: Buying and selling online over the Internet.

Export license: Government document that authorizes the export of specific goods in specific quantities to a particular destination. This document may be required for most or all exports to some countries or for other countries only under special circumstances.

Export management company (EMC): Company that performs the functions that would be typically performed by the export department or the international sales department of manufacturers and suppliers. EMCs develop personalized services promoting their clients' products to international buyers and distributors. They solicit and transact business in the names of the producers they represent or in their own name for a commission, salary, or retainer plus commission. EMCs usually specialize either by product or by foreign market. Because of their specialization, the best EMCs know their products and the markets they serve very well and usually have well-established networks of foreign distributors already in place. This immediate access to foreign markets is one of the principal reasons for using an EMC, because establishing a productive relationship with a foreign representative may be a costly and lengthy process.

Export packing list: List that itemizes the exported material in each package and indicates the type of package, such as a box, crate, drum, or carton. An export packing list is considerably more detailed and informative than a standard domestic packing list. It also shows the individual net, tare, and gross weights and measurements for each package (in both U.S. and metric systems).

Export processing zone (EPZ): Site in a foreign country established to encourage and facilitate international trade. EPZs include free trade zones, special economic zones, bonded warehouses, free ports, and customs zones. EPZs have evolved from initial assembly and simple processing activities to include high-tech and science parks, finance zones, logistics centers, and even tourist resorts.

Export quotas: Specific restrictions or ceilings imposed by an exporting country on the value or volume of certain exports designed, for example, to protect domestic producers and consumers from temporary shortages of the goods affected or to bolster their prices in world markets.

Export subsidies: Government payments or other financially quantifiable benefits provided to domestic producers or exporters contingent on the export of their goods and services.

Export trading company (ETC): Company that acts as an independent distributor, creating transactions by linking domestic producers and foreign buyers. As opposed to representing a given manufacturer in a foreign market, the ETC determines what U.S. products are desired in a given market and then works with U.S. producers to satisfy the demand. ETCs can perform a sourcing function, searching for U.S. suppliers to fill specific foreign requests for U.S. products.

FAS: Free alongside ship. This term refers to a seller's price for the goods, including the charge for delivery of the goods alongside at the named port of export. The seller handles the cost of wharfage, while the buyer is accountable for the costs of loading, ocean transportation, and insurance. It is the seller's responsibility to clear the goods for export.

FCA: Free carrier. FCA refers to a named place within the country of origin of the shipment. The terms define the seller's responsibility for handing over the goods to a named carrier at the named shipping point. According to *Incoterms 2000*, the named shipping point may be the seller's premises. In that case, it is the seller's responsibility to clear the goods for export from the United States. FCA may be used for any mode of transport.

FOB: An international commercial term (Incoterm) that means free on board and is used in international sales contracts. In an FOB contract, a buyer and a seller agree on a designated FOB point. The seller assumes the cost of having goods packaged and ready for shipment from the FOB point, whether it is the seller's own place of business or some intermediate point. The buyer assumes the costs and risks from the FOB point, including inland transportation costs and risks in the exporting country, as well as all subsequent transportation costs, including the costs of loading the merchandise on a vessel. If the contract stipulates "FOB vessel," the seller bears all transportation costs to the vessel named by the buyer, as well as the costs of loading the goods on that vessel. The same principle applies to the abbreviations FOR (free on rail) and FOT (free on truck).

Free in: Pricing term that indicates that the charterer of a vessel is responsible for the cost of loading goods onto the vessel.

Free in and out: Pricing term that indicates that the charterer of the vessel is responsible for the cost of loading and unloading goods from the vessel.

Free out: Pricing term that indicates that the charterer of the vessel is responsible for the cost of unloading goods from the vessel.

Foreign Corrupt Practices Act: Act making it unlawful for persons or firms subject to U.S. jurisdiction to offer, pay, or promise to pay money or anything of value to any foreign official for the purpose of obtaining or retaining business. It is also unlawful to make a payment to any person while knowing that all or a portion of the payment will be offered, given, or promised, directly or indirectly, to any foreign official for the purposes of assisting the firm in obtaining or retaining business. "Knowing" includes the concepts of "conscious disregard" and "willful blindness." The FCPA also covers foreign persons or firms that commit acts in furtherance of such bribery in the territory of the United States. U.S. persons or firms, or covered foreign persons or firms, should consult an attorney when confronted with FCPA issues.

Foreign-trade zones: Domestic U.S. sites that are considered outside U.S. customs territory and are available for activities that might otherwise be carried on overseas for customs reasons. For export operations, the zones provide accelerated export status for purposes of excise tax rebates. For reexport activities, no customs duties, federal excise taxes, or state or local ad valorem taxes are charged on foreign goods moved into zones unless and until the goods or products made from them are moved into customs territory. Thus, the use of zones can be profitable for operations involving foreign dutiable materials and components being assembled or produced in the United States for reexport.

Freight forwarder: Agent for moving cargo to an overseas destination. These agents are familiar with the import rules and regulations of foreign countries, the export regulations of the U.S. government, the methods of shipping, and the documents related to foreign trade.

Incoterms: *See terms of sale.*

Indirect exporting: Sale by the exporter to the buyer through a domestically located intermediary, such as an export management company or an export trading company.

Inspection certificate: Document required by some purchasers and countries to attest to the specifications of the goods shipped. The inspection is usually performed by a third party.

Insurance certificate: Document prepared by the exporter or freight forwarder to provide evidence that insurance against loss or damage has been obtained for the goods.

Intellectual property: Collective term used to refer to new ideas, inventions, designs, writings, films, and so on that are protected by a copyright, patent, or trademark.

Joint venture: Independent business formed cooperatively by two or more parent firms. This type of partnership is often used to avoid restrictions on foreign ownership and for longer-term arrangements that require joint product development, manufacturing, and marketing.

Letter of credit: Instrument issued by a bank on behalf of an importer that guarantees an exporter payment for goods or services, provided that the terms of the credit are met. A letter of credit issued by a foreign bank is sometimes confirmed by a U.S. bank. This confirmation means that the U.S. bank (the confirming bank) adds its promise to pay to that of the foreign bank (the issuing bank). A letter of credit may be either irrevocable, in which case it cannot be changed unless both parties agree, or revocable, in which case either party may unilaterally make changes. A revocable letter of credit is inadvisable as it carries many risks for the exporter.

Licensing: Arrangement in which a firm sells the rights to use its products or services but retains some control. Although not usually considered to be a form of partnership, licensing can lead to partnerships.

Market survey: Report that provides a narrative description and assessment of a particular market along with relevant statistics. The reports are often based on original research conducted in the countries studied and may include specific information on both buyers and competitors.

Packing list: *See export packing list.*

Patent: Right that entitles the patent holder, within the country that granted or recognizes the patent, to prevent all others, for a set period of time, from using, making, or selling the subject matter of the patent.

Piggyback marketing: Arrangement in which one manufacturer or service firm distributes a second firm's product or service. The most common piggybacking situation is when a U.S. company has a contract with an overseas buyer to provide a wide range of products or services. Often this first company does not produce all of the products it is under contract to provide, and it turns to other U.S. companies to provide the remaining products.

Primary market research: Collection of data directly from a foreign marketplace through interviews, surveys, and other direct contact with representatives and potential buyers. Primary market research has the advantage of being tailored to your company's needs and provides answers to specific questions, but the collection of such data is time consuming and expensive.

Pro forma invoice: Invoice prepared by the exporter before shipping the goods, informing the buyer of the goods to be sent, their value, and other key specifications.

Quotation: Offer by the exporter to sell the goods at a stated price and under certain conditions.

Remarketer: Export agent or merchant who purchases products directly from the manufacturer, packing and marking the products according to his or her own specifications. Remarketers then sell these products overseas through their contacts in their own names and assume all risks.

Sales representative: Representative who uses your company's product literature and samples to present the product to potential buyers. An overseas sales representative is the equivalent of a manufacturer's representative in the United States. The sales representative usually works on a commission basis, assumes no risk or responsibility, and is under contract for a definite period of time.

Secondary market research: Collection of data from various sources, such as trade statistics for a country or a product. Working with secondary sources is less expensive and helps your company focus its marketing efforts. Although secondary data sources are critical to market research, they do have limitations. The most recent statistics for some countries may be more than two years old, and the data may be too broad to be of much value to your company.

Shipper's export declaration (SED): Document used to control exports and act as a source document for official U.S. export statistics. SEDs, or their electronic equivalent, are required for shipments when the value of the commodities, classified under any single Schedule B number, is more than $2,500. SEDs must be prepared and submitted, regardless of value, for all shipments requiring an export license or destined for countries restricted by the Export Administration Regulations.

Sight draft: Document used when the exporter wishes to retain title to the shipment until it reaches its destination and payment is made. Before the shipment can be released to the buyer, the original "order" ocean bill of lading (the document that evidences title) must be properly endorsed by the buyer and surrendered to the carrier. It is important to note that air waybills do not need to be presented in order for the buyer to claim the goods. Thus, risk increases when a sight draft is being used with an air shipment.

Tariff: Tax imposed on a product when it is imported into a country. Some foreign countries apply tariffs to exports.

Technology licensing: Contractual arrangement in which the licenser's patents, trademarks, service marks, copyrights, trade secrets, or other intellectual property may be sold or made available to a licensee for compensation that is negotiated in advance between the parties. U.S. companies frequently license their technology to foreign companies that then use it to manufacture and sell products in a country or group of countries defined in the licensing agreement. A technology licensing agreement usually enables a firm to enter a foreign market quickly and poses fewer financial and legal risks than owning and operating a foreign manufacturing facility or participating in an overseas joint venture.

Terms of sale: Terms that define the obligations, risks, and costs of the buyer and seller involving the delivery of goods that comprise the export transaction. These terms are commonly known as *Incoterms*.

Time draft: Document used when the exporter extends credit to the buyer. The draft states that payment is due by a specific time after the buyer accepts the time draft and receives the goods. By signing and writing "accepted" on the draft, the buyer is formally obligated to pay within the stated time.

Trademark: Word, symbol, name, slogan, or combination thereof that identifies and distinguishes the source of sponsorship of goods and may serve as an index of quality of a particular product.

Trade statistics: Data that indicate total exports or imports by country and by product. They allow you to compare the size of the market for a product in various countries. By looking at statistics over several years, you can determine which markets are growing and which markets are shrinking.

Trading house: Company specializing in the exporting and importing of goods produced or provided by other companies.

Warehouse receipt: Receipt identifying the commodities deposited in a recognized warehouse. It is used to transfer accountability when the domestic carrier moves the export item to the port of embarkation and leaves it with the ship line for export.

www.ingramcontent.com/pod-product-compliance
Lightning Source LLC
Chambersburg PA
CBHW051706170526
45167CB00002B/560